MIDDLESBROUGH

1920 - 2020

A CENTURY OF CHANGE

Araf Chohan

Dedication

Today Middlesbrough is a truly progressive, cosmopolitan and international town with residents from every corner of the globe. I dedicate this book to all those who have chosen to make Middlesbrough their home town.

As a planned community in 1830 with no history, all of the original townsfolk of Middlesbrough were actually immigrants, coming initially from other parts of the country. They were quickly followed by people from all parts of the world who emigrated to the town. In fact, one of the most famous immigrants was our first MP, Henry William Ferdinand Bolckow, who came to Middlesbrough from Germany. Many other early industrialists followed suit.

Resident E. W. Hornung, the author of the A J Raffles series of stories about a gentleman thief, and brother-in-law to Sir Arthur Conan Doyle, was of Hungarian descent. Even our very own superstar Chris Rea's family were immigrants from Italy, and his mother of Irish heritage.

Yet the essence of all the ordinary people who made Middlesbrough their home were folk such as my parents and uncles who hailed from the Punjab in India. They were fiercely proud of their adopted home town, as was my dear friend Raja Asghar, a very proud 'smoggie' who came as a young boy in the early 1960s from Jhelum in Pakistan to Middlesbrough where sadly, aged only 61, he was laid to rest in August 2018.

First published 2019

ISBN 978 1 9996470 5 6

British Library Cataloguing-in-Publication Data
A catalogue record for this book is available from the British Library.

Published by Destinworld Publishing Ltd   **www.destinworld.com**

CONTENTS

INTRODUCTION

Middlesbrough's photographic history is well documented in many local history publications. However, many photographs seen here in this book have never been published before.

This rare collection of images, gathered mostly from my own personal collection as well as other sources, is seen together for the very first time to create this unique record of the last hundred years of Middlesbrough's history.

It has been incredibly difficult to choose from the many thousands of images in my collection. I have tried to only use previously unseen images that represent the decade in which they were taken. Despite how daunting the task has been, it is one I have relished in ensuring a unique and wonderfully evocative look at the last hundred years of the photographic history of the town.

It is impossible to cover the whole town and its many suburbs in detail, or to be fully comprehensive with views of all major buildings, such as all of the churches, schools and hospitals that have occupied the town. However, I have tried to include all major landmarks. In the confines of the book, however, this is a mere snapshot of the history of this town which grew up in the mid-1800s and has become one of the UK's leading digital and creative hubs, and home to a thriving university.

I love Middlesbrough. I was born in the town centre, in its heart, and still love it even after the destruction of its urban core. I love it because it is my home town, regardless of the march of time and the incredible changes over the decades covered in this book, which have left the town utterly unrecognisable in many ways.

Some 'Boro' folk I have known revisiting the town, having moved away to other parts of the world, have been totally shocked and amazed at the loss of not just the odd street here and there, but huge areas of the centre. Whole neighbourhoods have been demolished, not just during the 1960s and 70s, but continually to the present day with the Gresham area being the most recent.

The Middlesbrough that so many of a certain mature age knew simply no longer exists. The buildings, streets and neighbourhoods have all been consigned to the images in books like this, and will grow out of living memory soon enough.

As we pass through the ten decades here, I have gone into further detail about what has been lost and the changes that have occurred. It has been interesting to consider that what was seen as new in the earlier decades covered is now considered historic.

The changes have been seen all over the urban townscape, especially in and around the town centre and the old St Hilda's and dock areas. New names have emerged to give these areas a fresh, modern appeal – places like Middlehaven and the Boho Zone.

In the town centre, redevelopment of the retail fabric of the town saw new shopping centres spring up, tearing away huge parts of the old centre core of Victorian buildings and even whole streets.

Starting with the Dundas Shopping Centre and closely followed by The Cleveland Centre and Hill Street Centre, and much later the Captain Cook Square development, it turned Middlesbrough into the most important retail centre in the Tees Valley.

Vast new buildings have sprung up, like the Riverside Stadium, Middlesbrough College and the many parts of the Teesside University campus, plus a new police headquarters, medical research centre, leisure developments, housing, and the promise of a new snow centre in the next few years.

Teesside University itself, which was once Teesside Polytechnic, now spreads all over the town centre, growing and expanding in all directions with new buildings and student accommodation. It has become an important and successful academic institution.

The once mighty industrial area of the old Ironmasters District has also seen transformational developments, with all old industry now replaced by small modern business and light industrial units.

The A66 northern bypass was one of the most controversial construction projects. It carved its way through the once tightly-packed terraces of the Newport and Cannon Street areas, continuing eastwards through the town centre and its Victorian buildings on its way to North Ormesby, South Bank and Redcar.

Just outside of the town, the A19 and A174 "Parkway" added to the transport connectivity to this still relatively new town, giving access to the national motorway network.

Housing is also an area which has continually developed as Middlesbrough has grown. Private and council estates were built during every decade up to the present day, on every scrap of available land, marking a trend of moving outwards from the town centre. Communities have grown in places like Acklam, Berwick Hills, Eston, Linthorpe, Tollesby, Normanby, Ormesby, Coulby Newham and Marton

It is not only the physical changes that we have seen, but also the make up of the town's population which has moved from a homogeneous base to become an international melting pot, with new immigrants from across the globe joining older, more established communities, making Middlesbrough the cosmopolitan hub of the Tees Valley.

Such have been the incredible changes in Middlesbrough between 1920 and 2020. It has been a tremendous century of change for this town, the Infant Hercules, the youngest child of enterprise, which has grown to become the central hub of the Teesside conurbation.

Araf Chohan
September 2019

The 1920s

A 1926 image of the town centre looking southwards towards Albert Park. Middlesbrough here still clearly retains the grid pattern layout of the 19th Century Victorian town.

After the Great War of 1914-1918 a period of peace and calm returned. The "Roaring" 1920s experienced in London were not the same in the industrial heartlands of the north. Here in Middlesbrough menfolk arrived back from four years of bitter conflict to the land fit for heroes, but it was pretty much the same as when they had left.

Middlesbrough's Cenotaph honouring the fallen of World War I was unveiled on 11th November 1922 and was the first public monument since the statue of Sir Samuel Sadler in 1913.

However, major change was looming and Middlesbrough embarked upon its first ever comprehensive slum clearance scheme in the St Hilda's area, where old wynds and courtyards were demolished and new housing erected.

Further development on a much larger scale began in 1922. The green fields at Grove Hill, once one of the most salubrious suburbs on the edge of Middlesbrough, became the town's purpose-built Council Estate. This was preceded by the new Acklam Garden City at West Lane, close to the General Hospital and Linthorpe Cemetery. By the end of the decade the town had spread southwards far from its Victorian core north of Albert Park.

The town centre saw old music halls converting into cinemas and horse drawn carriages giving way to motor cars and buses, with Exchange Place becoming a public bus hub. Shops were redeveloped and enlarged, and smaller factories sprang up to complement the old heavy industry still lining the River Tees. The 1920s was a decade of peace, rebuilding and reconstruction.

The Transporter Bridge was, and still is, a unique mode of crossing over the River Tees. Opened in 1911 it is seen in this view in early 1920 some nine years after its opening. The suspended gondola is heading to the north bank at Port Clarence, where this picture is taken from. St Hilda's Church tower and the original township and quayside can be seen framed by the giant legs of the bridge. Much of these early dock areas were lost by the early 1980s as Teesport developed downstream with its larger and more modern facilities.

The River Tees was a very busy river in the 1920s compared to today. It was lined with heavy industry on both banks and shipping was abundant up and down the river, hence the reason for building the Transporter Bridge in a form that easily allowed vessels to enter and leave without hindrance.

This very nostalgic view of the river shows three tugs escorting a large ship. Taken from the top of the Transporter Bridge you can see the busy shipping and industrial landscape that has been lost with the decline of the town's once mighty iron, steel and shipbuilding industries.

Middlesbrough Dock opened in 1842 and is seen here in an early aerial view some 82 years later in 1924. There are over a dozen ships berthed showing just how busy the Dock was in its heyday, jam packed with shipping from across the globe, both importing and exporting goods.

Here can be seen one of the many larger ships being escorted and guided out of the narrow dock entrance by a Tees tug. This was a delicate operation since the dock was not really designed for such large vessels. The tower of the Town Hall can be glimpsed in the background on the left of the image whilst the prominent Dock Tower stands on the right.

New Bus Station, Middlesbrough

A small new bus station opened behind the Royal Exchange in 1925 with parallel queues which become known as the Corporation Bus Station. It is seen here before being replaced by an island structure which opened in 1937.

Hinton & Sons on the corner of Corporation Road and Albert Road (now the HSBC bank) was one of Middlesbrough's most popular and well known stores. Built in 1909, the site was originally Dr Grieve's School, part of which still survived into the early 1900s until it was demolished for the extension of the expanding Hinton's chain of stores. They had started off in the old town on South Street.

In 1928, severe flooding occurred in and around the North Ormesby and Borough Road area of the town. This view shows North Ormesby Road close to the Severn Street area, in a part of the town known as the 'Rivers' owing to the streets (on the left) being named after English rivers.

A very early 1920 view of North Ormesby Road looking towards the town centre. This rather gloomy image is probably quite authentic in its depiction of what it was actually like as the industrial grime and smoke permeated all around the area. Smokeless zones were still more than 50 years away.

Public houses were such an integral part of Middlesbrough life and every part of the town had its "local" pub. One was never very far from these establishments, especially in the old town.

The Captain Cook public house seen here in this 20s view. It was opened in 1846 and is the last intact surviving pub in St. Hilda's, and the oldest in Middlesbrough. The older Ship Inn building from 1831, although still standing, is in a very derelict and perilous state following a fire.

A fantastic photograph of the very grand Leeds Hotel in the late 1920s prior to it being bombed on 26th August 1942, which left it almost destroyed. What remained after this devastating Nazi air raid was demolished. The site on the corner of Linthorpe Road and Wilson Street is now occupied by the A66 flyover.

The Erimus Hotel at 33 Fletcher Street on the corner with Newton Street. It was opened in 1880, and the building was demolished for the construction of the Cleveland Centre in the 1960s, although the name lived on for a while with new premises inside the shopping centre.

The Palmerston opened in 1869 on the corner of Newport Road and Lord Street. This wonderfully evocative image is looking down Newport Road towards the town centre. On the left of the image stand two policemen, one being an inspector; something has caught their eye as they look on somewhat avidly.

A busy late 1920s view of Newport Road looking east towards Corporation Road. The scene shows Manfield's departmental store on the right which became Binns and was burnt down in 1942. It was replaced by the present Binns/House of Fraser Building.

A view of Newport Road looking towards the town centre with St. Paul's Church on the right. Here in the late 1920s trams still ran on the route to Norton, but buses had also begun to make their appearance alongside them. The trams would become obsolete by the start of the next decade.

Marches and marching bands were commonplace in the 1920s as illustrated here in these two wonderful images. The cavalcade is entering Victoria Square from Russell Street which can been seen stretching out beyond towards St. John's Church at its junction with Marton Road. Vast crowds were common for all major events particularly as much of the population lived in the town centre.

Albert Road - the premier thoroughfare linking the railway station to the town - can be seen here looking north from the corner of Grange Road. Near the Town Hall are two double decker trams, and in the foreground a car and a bike are both heading down towards its junction with Grange Road.

Another view of Albert Road in the mid-1920s. We see a motor bus swirling around into Grange Road heading for Stockton, sharing the road with the trams until the last one ran in 1934.

In this incredible view of Linthorpe Road looking north from just past Southfield Road we can see the busy urban townscape showing the old St. George's Church with its looming tower on the left and the then Royal Opera House, which later became the Gaumont Cinema, dominating the corner plot on the right.

Just a little further down from the previous photograph and still looking north up Linthorpe Road is another fabulous image taken by the eminent local photographer Haig Parry. In the view the Empire Hotel can be seen on the right and the road is full of people out on what seems like a nice sunny day judging by the number of awnings that are opened out.

A lovely ensemble of images showing the departmental store Dickson & Benson.

The Linthorpe Road exterior and main entrance to the store.

The latest up-to-date 1920s fashion in the window displays.

The interior of the store with the haberdashery and glove departments. The seated lady could be a customer or a very smartly dressed shop assistant.

Electric trams were a feature on the streets of Middlesbrough from their opening on 16th July 1898 till their demise on 9th June 1934. During the 1920s they were at their peak with both single and double decker trams in operation. Double deckers ran along Newport and North Ormesby Roads and both types ran along Albert Road from the station to the Linthorpe Terminus at Roman Road. Single decker trams only ran along the Albert Road section south of the station under the railway bridge to the Transporter.

The following tram images in the mid-1920s were commissioned for the 1926 Middlesbrough Pictorial Industrial Book.

A rare view of the overhead wires seen here with front of a double decker tram on Newport Road at Newhouse's Corner.

A single decker
near Park Road
North.

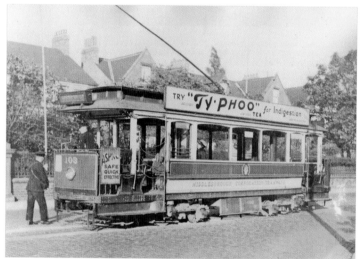

A single decker
on The Avenue
near the Roman
Road terminus.

A marvellous
view looking
down upon
the top deck of
double decker
on Albert Road
close to its
junction with
Grange Road.
The Town Hall
clock tower and
the old Victoria
Square trees are
quite dominant.

A tram depot of 14,250 square yards was built in Parliament Road and formally opened on 19th July 1921 by the chairman of the Council Tramways Committee, Councillor Edwin Turner.

Seen here in 1921 soon after the official opening, showing the exterior on Parliament Road.

The interior of the tram depot with both double decker and single decker trams all lined up and ready for their daily runs.

The 1925 Carnival Week was the first ever in Middlesbrough's history and was a major fundraising event, organized primarily to raise money for the town's hospitals. Streets, vehicles, floats and even fire engines were all fantastically decorated for the event and the whole town was fully engaged in a fabulous week of festivities

A wonderful view of Wilson Street looking towards Linthorpe Road with crowds milling around. The A66 viaduct stands on the site of the buildings on the right today.

A decorated truck in Dunning Road.

A very crowded Newport Road with vast number of people watching the long parade.

One of the Council's fire engines in the Town Hall's Quadrangle ready to join other decorated vehicles.

A nautical scene outside the Railway Station on Albert Road. One of the more unusual modes of transport on display.

Hazel Street looking north towards Corporation Road showing the extent that ordinary streets were involved in the carnival. Most were vying to be the best decorated street.

This fantastic aerial view of the town centre looking north in late 1929 shows the Constantine College building in the final stages of its construction and which was opened the following year. The High School is centre bottom and Hugh Bell Schools can be seen in full, fronting Victoria Square at the centre. At the extreme bottom right is the old St. Hilda's Vicarage which became the site of the new Evening Gazette building in the following decade.

The newly built Number 16 Branch of the Middlesbrough Co-operative Society was located on the corner of Linthorpe Road and Devonshire Road. The building still stands (currently the Olivello restaurant) but is mostly unrecognizable.

In 1926 the old Blue Hall in Linthorpe was demolished and Shipman's Bakery and neighbouring houses were subsequently built on the site. Seen here from the Linthorpe Cemetery, the Hall stands behind the large crowd who were involved in clearing the area of trees during a time of great hardship and unemployment. The building shown here was a later hall built on the same site as the original Blue Hall which was demolished around 1869.

An evocative view of Oxford Road photographed by the well-established local photographer Haig Parry, taken near the one-time petrol filling station, previously the old Olympia skating rink. The Roman Road junction is beyond at the end of the row of houses on the right. Parry's own motorcar DC1854 was often used in the scenes he photographed, as here in this mid-1920s postcard image.

Taken around 1923/24 the row of shops at Belle Vue, as can be clearly seen displayed on the building on the right, were constructed in 1909 at the end of the Edwardian period. At the time, they were in the countryside right on the edge of town in what was the very salubrious area known as "Grove Hill", which was home to the rich and famous of the town.

Seen here soon after its completion in the early 1920s, the Grove Hill estate was a place where modern homes with gardens were built. These were indeed homes fit for heroes who had fought in World War I and returned to live in decent houses which were a far cry from the often squalid Victorian terraces of St. Hilda's, from where many had come.

In this marvellous stereoscopic view taken looking at the Palladium roundabout, Valley Road is on the extreme left, in the centre is Bishopton Road, and Marton Burn Road is to the right. They all converge with Eastbourne Road, out of shot behind the camera.

Marton Burn Road was one of the main arterial roads in the new suburb of Grove Hill and was also one of the first to be served by motor buses. The image seen here shows the road looking very new and empty, towards its junction with Marton Road near Belle View.

In this lovely view we see an early motor bus operating the Middlesbrough Corporation "C" route to town, together with a wonderful looking car and traditional old horse and cart, soon set to disappear from the urban scene.

Many thousands of old photographs exist of the exterior of our grand old buildings, but very few are published of the interiors of those very same buildings. The images that follow are rare, as they show the long-forgotten interiors of some well-known Middlesbrough landmarks.

The Scala Cinema opened on Newport Road on 17th May 1920 and was taken over by Associated British Cinemas (ABC) in December 1935, but closed on 22nd April 1940. It was re-opened with its original name by the Plaza Cinema (Newsham) Ltd. group but closed for good in April 1961. Shown here is the inside of the Scala Cinema in 1927.

The Elite Picture House's Sparks Café on Linthorpe Road was a genteel meeting place where one could relax and have afternoon tea in a pleasant and convivial environment.

The 1930s

Great crowds throng Borough Road on 2nd July 1930 at the opening of Constantine Technical College by HRH The Prince of Wales, later King Edward VIII. This was a great public occasion and the first royal visit since World War I.

The 1930s started with the first royal visit to Middlesbrough since the 1917 morale-boosting visit of their majesties King George V and Queen Mary during World War I. Their son and heir (later King Edward VIII) came to the town to open Constantine College on 2nd July 1930. This was the largest Higher Education institution to be built since before the war and the whole town was in a frenzy of excitement. An even larger royal visit occurred just four years later when the then Duke and Duchess of York (the Future King George VI and Queen Elizabeth) came to open the Tees (Newport) Vertical Lift Bridge in February 1934.

Significant buildings constructed during the 1930s include the Odeon cinema on Corporation Road, York House on Borough Road and the former National Westminster Bank on Albert Road. Many new places of worship were also constructed, such as the Sacred Heart Catholic twin tower church (1934), and the now Seventh Day Adventist Chapel (1935); both on Linthorpe Road. Further out in Whinney Banks, St Francis Church and St Joseph's Church on Marton Road, Grove Hill, opened in the mid-30s.

On the southern fringes of town in Longlands, Linthorpe and Acklam, private semi-detached homes so typical of 1930s suburban Britain were constructed in great numbers. Further expansion of Grove Hill and the new Whinney Banks council estates also occurred in the once open fields of West Lane and Acklam.

The interwar years were a time of hope and change after the carnage of World War I. Middlesbrough expanded well beyond the original settlement north of the railway line. This new age dawned and sprang a town of homes with gardens, and new modern public buildings considered fresh and stylish, totally different to their fussy Victorian and Edwardian predecessors. This was the 'modern' Middlesbrough of the 1930s.

A clear view of the new Constantine College seen here in 1931 at an unusual angle looking from the corner of Albert Road, showing the imposing Borough Road frontage.

Another wonderful view of the college seen here in 1932 with the old Middlesbrough High School also in full view. Although both buildings survive, the High school, which opened in 1877, has lost an entire wing to the left of the tower; the rest remains and is now a listed building - one of the few Victorian buildings of historic merit left in Middlesbrough's town centre.

An early aerial photograph covering most of the central area of Middlesbrough town centre. All of the town's major landmarks can clearly be seen. The busy industries of the north bank of the Tees are visible to the north.

The new Corporation Bus Station which opened in October 1931 is seen here a year later. It replaced an earlier terminus. Buses were to totally replace the trams by 1934 and were more numerous, running on routes which the trams had never reached such as the new estates of Grove Hill and Whinney Banks.

Newport Road looking towards Corporation Road. In this early 30s image, on the right is Manfield's Store and on the left Newhouse's, whilst an early motorbus is seen outside the store running along the tram tracks which were soon to be made redundant.

A view in 1930 of Corporation Road looking towards the Town Hall, showing this part of the town which contained all the larger department stores and was a busy thoroughfare of trams and vehicles. Shopping crowds can be seen milling around in great numbers.

The Scala cinema was one of the earliest in Middlesbrough and opened on Monday, 17th May 1920. In this late 1939 postcard view the cinema can be seen on its prominent corner site at Hill Street and Newport Road. The rest of the scene shows the view looking towards Linthorpe Road.

A lovely old postcard view of Newport Road looking towards the town from the Tees Bridge entrance, showing the Newport public house which opened in 1867 on the corner with Samuelson Street.

This very clear 1930s photograph of Albert Road looking north shows the Town Hall in all its Gothic Victorian grandeur. Not as busy as today's roads but still an important thoroughfare, Albert Road is the main link to the railway station and the Transporter Bridge.

A 1932 view of Albert Road taken further south than the previous image, still looking north. This is a more unusual photographic view not often seen from the junction with Borough Road.

Linthorpe Road in 1933 with the wall of St. Barnabas' Church on the left. A fairly tranquil scene as opposed to today's busy road, with just the odd car in view but plenty of pedestrians.

The North Riding Infirmary, seen here on a wet and gloomy day in the mid-1930s, was a local landmark since the early 1860s. It was much lamented upon its closure in 2003 and the subsequent outcry failed to stop it from being demolished. It was subsequently replaced by an Aldi store and a Travelodge hotel.

Huge crowds gather around the last tram on its final run down to the Parliament Road Depot on 9th June 1934. Operating since 1898, it was a sad day for the once popular mode of transport which had been replaced by the more flexible buses, which had a more extensive route network and were much more viable and versatile for the transport of the general public.

Small shops like here at 76, Linthorpe Road had thrived since Victorian times, but larger departmental stores began dominating the town centre and by the 1930s they were being extended to become even larger. The second picture here shows the new extension of Newhouse's.

A 1930s postcard of the Joe Walton's youth club on Lower Feversham Street. This night-time view is of the original building which was sadly demolished in 2018. Joe Walton's was a well-established and very popular youth club and although the original building survived till only recently, the youth club itself lived on having moved many years ago from its original premises.

Middlesbrough Fire Station, seen here soon after its official opening in 1939, was the first purpose-built station in the town. Although now demolished and replaced by an up-to-date and more modern building, the original tower has been retained as a piece of the town's history.

Middlesbrough has always celebrated special occasions with great displays of public support for all the important events in the town's history, from royal visits to local celebrations. In the past, special events such as coronations and jubilees were particular favourites and streets were beautifully decorated.

This photograph of Alma Street in the St. Hilda's area of the town shows it decorated for the Silver Jubilee celebrations of the 25th anniversary of the reign of King George V in May 1935.

Albert Road beautifully decorated for the King's Jubilee like many other important thoroughfares in the town.

This lovely and unique view of the Town Hall shows it actually in the process of being decorated and prepared for the coming festivities.

A statue of King George V was erected at the Town Hall entrance for the Jubilee. The entrance itself was also festooned and decorated with portraits of the King and Queen with a huge crown and garlands in red, white and blue.

One of the most important royal visits to the town was during this decade for the opening of the Tees (Newport) Bridge on 28th February 1934 by the Duke and Duchess of York (the future king George VI and Queen Elizabeth). The bridge was only the second crossing of the River Tees in Middlesbrough.

The series of images that follow depict this very important event of the 1930s.

The old Newport railway station is in the foreground with the streets that were demolished for the approach to the bridge in the background. St. Cuthbert's Church can also be seen in the centre background of the picture.

The bridge's approach roadway under construction.

Newport Bridge under construction.

The completed bridge with the vertical lift roadway in both the down and up positions.

The royal couple are seated outside the Town Hall in their motor car ready to drive to the bridge for its official opening, having arrived by train from London.

The bridge approach roads crowds awaiting the royal party.

The royal cavalcade enters the bridge approach.

The 1940s

One of the most damaging periods of World War II for Middlesbrough was the daylight raid on the railway station on the August bank holiday of 1942. The raid culminated in the partial destruction of the station's roof and heavy damage to the northern platforms and associated station buildings. The raid killed eight people and injured 58. Psychologically it was a huge blow to the morale of the town.

For obvious reasons the 1940s were a time for rebuilding owing to the war years. There was a need to reconstruct many of the bombed-out homes, streets and public buildings, and clear the debris of various air raids and attacks.

Many buildings that were damaged, such as the Grand Hotel on Zetland Road, survived in a truncated form. However, the well-known Leeds Hotel had to be demolished, along with much of Wilson Street and surrounding areas near the Railway Station. Not all buildings that were damaged or lost were due to the war, however. The flagship Binns store on the prominent corner of Linthorpe and Newport roads was completely lost to arson in 1942.

Although Middlesbrough suffered losses to its infrastructure, it was minimal compared to the mass destruction of cities such as London, Liverpool, Bristol and Coventry. Considering the amount of heavy industry along its riverbanks and the importance of its docks and steelworks, it is incredible that it was not targeted in any major way.

Life had continued during the war years and there were a number of new construction projects. The Art-Deco style Co-Operative Building at 251-255 Linthorpe Road opened in 1941 (it survives to this day). The site was once home to the wooden church of St Aiden's which was demolished for the new store, replaced by a brick church in nearby Clifton Street.

On the Southern outskirts of the town, the council constructed the Thorntree Estate in 1947. Despite rationing and war, the town was still expanding as workers moved into employment in the heavy industries.

On a personal note, October 1949 saw the arrival in Middlesbrough of my very young and awestruck mother. Coming from the warm and sunny Punjab in India, she recalls arriving initially at Liverpool and her first sight of a grim, cold, wet and bombed city. Middlesbrough in 1949 was no different;quite an eye opener to the young Nafees Chohan who was to make her home in Grange Road for the next 61 years.

A marvellous and illuminating image of the remains of the Vulcan Street Salt Works complex. The Vulcan Street wall which remains today can't be seen in the photograph as it is still intact as part of the long building in the image with the damaged roof, of which it was once integral.

The River Tees seen here with the Newport Bridge and the heavy industry which once lined the river banks. The image is looking upstream towards Stockton, with the Middlesbrough bank on the left.

This lovely view of a large ship being towed by a tug in Middlesbrough was taken by the celebrated local photographer Haig Parry. Many large dock cranes can be seen lined up in the background, and one can just make out the Town Hall clock, centre left between the two funnels of the tug.

A fantastic photograph of a train locomotive engine being hoisted on to the Brecia in Middlesbrough Dock.

The oldest public house in Middlesbrough was the Ship Inn on Stockton Street, seen here in an image from the late 1940s. Now burnt out and derelict shell, the Ship Inn from 1831 was built at the earliest beginnings of Middlesbrough's inception, only a year earlier.

Located on the corner of Feversham Street and Cleveland Street, the Cleveland Bay Hotel was opened in 1846 and was one of the earliest to be licensed in the town. Seen here in the late 1940s, this hotel had a very domestic appearance almost like a double fronted terraced house.

Wilson Street looking towards Albert Road from the back of the Royal Exchange, seen here during the World War II years. The area was badly damaged by enemy bombing, however, this stretch of the street escaped the bombs as they fell on the section between Albert Road and Linthorpe Road.

Winterschladen & Co's wine and spirit merchants was a household name, and their premises in the under croft of the Railway Station also escaped any lasting damage during the devastating daylight air raid on the station during the 1942 August bank holiday.

A view of the Gilkes Street municipal swimming baths. They included the Slipper Baths which were used by generations of the townsfolk usually on a weekly basis.

A view of the Scala cinema on Newport Road from across the street looking westwards. The Scala was opened in 1920, but was to close in April 1961 as many of the older cinemas were unable to make a profit with the advent of television and other leisure pursuits. Also, larger purpose-built cinemas such as the Elite, Odeon and Majestic were more popular with the paying public.

A wonderfully busy Corporation Road seen here in the late 1940s looking westwards towards Linthorpe Road. The photograph shows the rather grand Corporation Hotel which dominates its commanding site at the corner of Albert Road. The brick structure on the left in the front of the Town Hall was the public conveniences which were handy in times of need when there were few such places available.

Almost every building depicted in this postcard view of Linthorpe Road has now been demolished, except for Newhouse Corner (now Debenhams) towards the end of the row of buildings on the left. All the structures on the right made way for the Cleveland Centre and Woolworths replaced much of the row of Victorian shops on the left. Now a pedestrianized shopping street it is hard to imagine it used to have two-way vehicular traffic as well as the general public in vast numbers. Then, as now, it was the premier shopping thoroughfare in the town.

Elite Cinema and Linthorpe Road, Middlesbrough.

This old postcard view is of Linthorpe Road looking in the direction of Tower House. This major landmark has now gone, replaced by a McDonald's restaurant. Most of the scene shown is fairly intact today, but much altered with more modern frontages. The lovely corner building facing the camera is currently a Greek restaurant. The postcard sender has added some helpful details about their life in Middlesbrough.

The Victoria Hall, a building which is seen here as the Middlesbrough Co-operative Society, was a major casualty of the Luftwaffe bombing raid on 25th July 1942 which also saw Turner's decorating store and Armstrong's garage destroyed.

An unusual image but quite a nice record of the more mundane things that were going on even during wartime. Here the statue of John Vaughan in Victoria Square is being cleaned and restored by workmen on what seems like a misty or smoky morning.

St. Luke's hospital was the town's institution for the care of the mentally ill, opened on 15th June 1898. It was a sprawling complex of buildings in its extensive grounds. Built in the Victorian period it was an "Asylum for those of an unsound mind" - something which is now consigned to the history books. At the time it was highly regarded and respected. It was situated on the edge of town along Marton Road in what was then countryside. Renamed Roseberry Park it is now a modern medical facility.

War preparations during the 1940s were numerous. All over the town the placing of sandbags around public buildings was taking place, with the public showing support for the protection of their town.

The Marsh Road recreation ground busy with volunteers working for the war effort.

This is a rare photograph of the preparations for the war effort with sand bagging in progress on the Town Hall frontage along Dunning Street in 1940. The view is looking north towards Corporation Road, with the Central Hotel just visible on the left beyond the Town Hall.

Workers in Corporation Road and Albert Road placing sandbags and other protections around the Town Hall.

This remarkable photograph of a municipal fire engine is a fine example of the fire fighting appliances that were in use during the war. This quite beautiful fire engine is parked in the Town Hall Quadrangle, where the town's fire station was once located. Three senior fire fighters stand proud alongside.

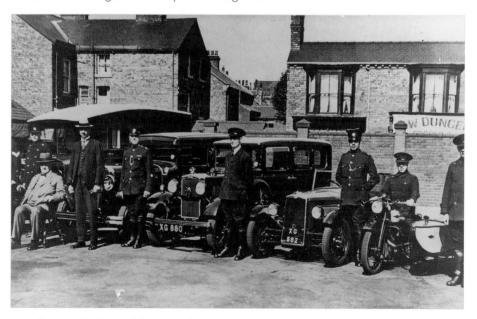

Equally proud, the Middlesbrough police constabulary are displaying their vehicles including a side car motorbike in the grounds of the High School. They have purposely lined them up from largest to smallest order.

Although a war was raging and bombs were falling, there were still normal fires and damaged buildings which were unrelated to the war. What made these fires worse was that they were actually crimes such as arson and were perpetuated on a town already suffering the hardships of a global conflict. Known as the great fire scare of March and June 1942, several stores were set alight. Binns was reduced to rubble in March and was later demolished, as seen in this image. Others stores such as Dickson & Benson and Uptons also suffered. The mystery was solved when a schoolboy was found attempting to push burning paper through the letter box of another store.

The Southfield Road Baptist Church opened in 1928, but due to structural faults was demolished in 1956. The adjoining church hall survived for a short time but eventually the whole site was redeveloped and the Salvation Army building now occupies the site.

Large parades were frequent in Middlesbrough during the period covered, from coronations and royal visits to carnivals and religious occasions, as can be seen here in these two wonderful images.

A huge parade along Linthorpe Road close to Southfield Road, with one of the original Uptons stores on the right.

A vast parade with bands, the police and fire department in full regalia marching along Corporation Road close to the Empire Theatre.

A very peaceful and serene view of the Cenotaph and Park Methodist Church on Linthorpe Road. The Cenotaph was unveiled to the public during the Armistice Day commemoration on 11th November 1922 outside Albert Park.

A rare view of a part of Linthorpe Road not normally photographed. The view is looking north just beyond the Dorman Museum, out of view behind the trees on the right. Also on the right are the twin towers of the Catholic Sacred Heart Church. On the left is the small but lovely Presbyterian / United Reformed Church of 1924, located on the corner of Clive Road. Park Methodist Church completes the trio in the distance.

Middlesbrough Fire Station on Park Road South seen here in the late 1940s. This building was replaced by a more modern facility in 2014, though the original tower of 1939 was retained.

The old Union Workhouse from 1878 which was on St. Barnabas Road in Linthorpe, was a local landmark that later became Holgate Municipal Hospital. It became part of the Middlesbrough General Hospital complex in early 1943. The view here is from the late 40s and shows the Victorian tower and main central building. However, by the mid-1980s demolition began on the old Holgate buildings and private housing was eventually built.

An aerial view of St. Luke's Hospital complex seen here in its entirety surrounded by fields, giving it a very rural aspect even though it was just on the edge of town. Marton Road is just visible at lower right.

The Ormesby Bungalow on a wet day during the war years. This was once a popular Edwardian café close to Marton Hall. By the time this rare image was taken it had become a busy petrol station. A café restaurant was still in operation, but more as a place for travellers rather than a place to visit.

The 1950s

A lovely view of Victoria Square seen here in the late 1950s with the terraced houses on Dunning Road still attached to the imposing Central Library. The Grange Road United Methodist Church dating from 1877 dominates the south eastern corner of the square beyond the library.

This was the decade of my birth, right in the middle of town in the downstairs back room of 185 Grange Road, on 27th October 1952. I can lay claim to having been truly born and bred in Middlesbrough. The decade actually began with the birth of my elder brother - the first of our family born in Britain since the arrival of my father in 1937. However, since there were no other Punjabi family ladies in Middlesbrough, my father sent my mum to our nearest relatives in Nottingham, where Bari was born on 30th September 1950. My sister, however, was born in Middlesbrough exactly one year prior to myself on 27th October 1951.

This was to be the Decade of Plenty as the then Conservative Prime Minister Harold Macmillan made in a now famous speech, in which he stated "Let us be frank about it, most of our people, have never had it so good." On the whole he was right, as anything was better than the war years, which was plain for all to see.

During my childhood I can still recall the gas lamplighters and various traders still using horse power, such as the coalman, the milkman, the furniture removers and the rag and bone man. Motorized vehicles were fast taking over.

Little was to change in the town centre until the end of the decade when major schemes came to fruition, turning it into the largest retail centre in the area. This began with the huge new Binns department store built on the site of its predecessor in 1957. The seven-storey Art Deco store was the largest in the area, and the height of modernity.

Not to be outdone, and on an equally prominent site opposite Binns on the corner of Linthorpe and Corporation roads, British Home Stores demolished the "Big Wesley" Chapel to make way for their large department store which opened on 2nd October 1958. Further along Linthorpe Road, Woolworths replaced their 1926 store of joined up terraced shops into a modern store, opening in late 1959.

Four estates began construction in the 1950s, in Berwick Hills (1951), Park End (1953), followed by Brambles Farm and then Pallister Park (1955) and Easterside (1956). An incredible number of houses were needed for the ever-expanding town with its growing population.

By the Late 50s the original town, now known as St. Hilda's (but more commonly referred to as "Over the Border"), was perceived by many to be a complete slum. There was no doubt in anyone's mind that the original Middlesbrough was in terminal decline and, sadly, wholesale demolition loomed.

The quayside just upstream from the Transporter Bridge which can be glimpsed in the background. The ship docked is called the Veenenburgh whose run was from Rotterdam to Middlesbrough. A cargo of timber is stacked on the dock.

Although built in the days of horses, carts and early motor vehicles, the Transporter Bridge was so well designed that it can easily transport modern cars, trucks and even double decker buses. Here we can see a Middlesbrough Corporation double decker bus with Billingham on its destination board.

St Hilda's Parish Church, seen here in 1955, was one of Middlesbrough's oldest places of worship and the first purpose-built Anglican church. It opened on 15th May 1840. Three other nonconformist church buildings preceded it. As the town's population moved south, St. Hilda's closed and was ultimately demolished in 1969.

A rare image showing the burnt-out shell of the Binns department store which was destroyed by a schoolboy arsonist in 1942. This view from 1955 shows the remains of the building looking down Linthorpe Road, with a large sign pointing customers towards the temporary premises which were located at 72-80 Corporation Road. These were used in the 1940s and 1950s until the new store we see today opened on the original site on 14th March 1957.

The Marks & Spencer store seen here in the mid-1950s was at this time quite a small concern. Located at 45 Linthorpe Road since its opening in 1901, the larger store that we see today was not opened until 1958. This was after several extensions elsewhere on Linthorpe Road.

A 1959 photograph showing the Newport Road frontage of Newhouse's department store. The buildings to the left of the store here have all been demolished and replaced by nondescript modern edifices. The loss especially of the three storey building immediately to left of Newhouse's was a needless destruction of yet another of the town's valuable Victorian heritage.

The two images here show Zetland Road which fronts the railway station. Although bombed in World War II, the row of buildings mostly survived and are much admired and of full of architectural merit.

The Zetland Hotel has one of the best preserved pub interiors in the country, which can still be seen today as part of the modern restaurant.

The Co-Operative Permanent Building Society's premises on Albert Road was located next door to the then Hintons large flagship store. The building now houses a retail store.

A different view of the entrance to Hintons Café which was a very popular venue to meet at for a snack, afternoon tea or a meal. The cafe had been in operation since the company's move to the huge store at the corner of Albert Road and Corporation Road. The building and this entrance are now incorporated into the HSBC bank.

A 1952 photograph of Borough Road. This building still exists as The Bottled Note and Harriet's, but is much altered. The lovely upstairs bay windows are still recognizable, however. The house next door is today a retail unit with an unsympathetic square frontage now replacing the grand London-style porticos.

The Co-operative Society Emporium building seen here in the early 50s from a unique angle, thanks to the cleared site opposite. Now beautifully restored thus making a fantastic change from the more usual Middlesbrough obsession of demolishing lovely old buildings for redevelopment. Currently housing a supermarket, betting shop and sports bar on the ground floor, fronting Linthorpe Road.

All Saints' Church and the now demolished church hall seen here in the summer of 1952. The poster displayed on the hall is advertising the film "Belles On Their Toes" showing at the Odeon, as well as a baby competition (note the many prams parked outside the church!).

A Closer look at Grange Road shows the old tram lines still clearly visible even though the last tram ran in 1934. The unloved Church House office block now stands on the site of the church hall but thankfully the church still survives in its original state.

Newport Road near to Hill Street here seen from a mid-1950s postcard is fairly animated but not too busy. At this time car ownership was not very widespread and a few bus routes ran along the street, which was the main road to Thornaby and Stockton. Hardy & Co was a local furniture store, and the new Binns building can be seen on the right. In-between, the sign for Grand Electric is just visible. This cinema had a 46-year run, opening in 1911 and closing in 1957, not too long after the photograph was taken.

Another rare postcard from my collection showing Linthorpe Road at the junction with Borough Road looking north towards the Wright's Tower House department store. A 'D' bus is pulled up at the bus stop.

Another truly fine view of 1950s Linthorpe Road, again looking north towards the town centre. The wonderful shop fronts on display run down from the Elite cinema and, although they are all still standing at the time of writing, the first three are soon to be demolished for access to a planned students' village on land behind the cinema in what is known as the Gresham area.

Two fantastic and rare views of the north side of Princes Road. The first is looking down towards Gresham Road from close to Walpole Street. The second is looking down towards Diamond Road from roughly the same spot. Both are largely devoid of vehicular traffic, unlike today where there are parked vehicles on both sides of the road. Most of the houses in this area have now been demolished.

Two nice looking Middlesbrough Fire Brigade appliances are parked in Southfield Road close to what was Martins Bank (now the TS One bar and restaurant) and in front of what is now Al Forno Restaurant.

The St. John's Garage of Pallister, Yare & Cobb Ltd. was in the building located on Marton Road with its junction with Grange Road East. The building still stands today, recently operating as a hairdresser. The upper pediment with the name has now been removed, however.

This 1958 photograph is a marvellous view of the well-known part of North Ormesby Road and what was a very well used railway crossing. This busy road linked the town centre to North Ormesby. No fewer than five double- and two single-decker buses can be seen here, together with numerous cars. It is testament to the need of a flyover, which was eventually built more than a decade later.

A clear view of the stunning Victorian houses of West Terrace in North Ormesby, seen here a decade or so before their demolition. West Terrace was the premier place to reside in the Victorian era and they were also the largest houses in North Ormesby, standing three floors above ground along with large, habitable basements.

These two wonderful photographs of the Odeon Cinema on Corporation Road show the cinema in all its original Art Deco glory. Opened on 25th February 1939, some 6 months before the outbreak of World War II, the Odeon sadly closed in June 2001. It was a popular night out in its heyday in the 1950s and 60s.

The film "Jacqueline", released in 1951, is being advertised in the first image. The second shows a closer view of the marvellous main entrance, with "A Place in the Sun", released in 1956, being shown.

The Elite cinema, later the ABC, and most recently The Crown pub, is a rare survivor, but its future is uncertain as it lies vacant and unused at the time of writing. Plans to bring a new use to this lovely building from 1923 will hopefully come to fruition.

The full corner aspect of the cinema. It is showing the famous 1951 film "A Streetcar Named Desire" as its main feature.

A fantastic overview of the Russell Street area looking northwards towards Middlesbrough Dock. Taken looking down Poplar and Pine streets, there are four major landmarks that can be seen. From left to right, they are the Transporter Bridge, the steeple of the Unitarian Church, the Star and Garter Hotel and the Odeon Cinema.

A lovely close view of the entrance of the Gaumont cinema on Linthorpe Road which was once Middlesbrough's Grand Opera house of 1903. It was converted in 1930 and lasted 34 years until it closed in 1964. It remained empty for many years before being demolished and replaced with a typical and uninspiring red brick office development of little merit whatsoever.

A wider view of the corner site of the once iconic Middlesbrough landmark Gaumont and Opera House building.

Linthorpe Road with the Gaumont on the left, and a busy scene looking southwards with a fire engine on display. A crowd is milling around, and a 'P' bus is stationary at the Gaumont bus stop.

The Dorman Museum located at the Albert Park entrance on Linthorpe Road has always been one of Middlesbrough and Teesside's premier museums. Some of the most popular exhibits were the collection of stuffed wild African animals and a huge collection of birds.

One of the two most popular of these was the lion and his zebra kill, which had thrilled children for many decades until it became unfashionable. In the second picture, staff members negotiate the famous bear on the steps of the museum during its removal for restoration.

Ayresome Park football ground was opened in 1903 and, after its closure was used as a training ground until it was demolished in early 1997. Middlesbrough Football Club moved to the new Riverside Stadium on 25th August 1995; it was the first stadium to be built after the Taylor Report which recommended that major stadiums should be all-seater. This very detailed 1950s aerial photograph shows Ayersome Park surrounded by the tightly packed terraced houses so typical of industrial Middlesbrough.

A view from the rooftop of the new Binns store. This 1959 scene overlooks the Hill Street area of the town, with the murky view a result of the pollution from the vast industries. It was not until the implementation of smokeless zones in the 1970s that the air cleared, consigning such scenes to history.

This series of wonderful images shows Queen Elizabeth's visit to Middlesbrough in 1956, which was the major occasion of the decade, and also the first time that the Queen visited the town. Huge crowds lined the streets to get a glimpse of Her Majesty and I, as a 4-year-old, was on Marton Road with my mum, dad, elder brother and sister to see the her pass, but I only have vague memories.

The Town Hall all decorated for the visit as viewed from the Hugh Bell School on the south side of the Victoria Square.

The Town Hall facade on Corporation Road equally decorated.

A remarkable view of the huge crowds on Corporation Road waiting for the Queen's arrival.

Dignitaries standing outside the Town Hall as Her Majesty arrives.

A rare image from my private collection showing crowds watching the Queen passing Marton Road School.

The Royal party passing the new Marton Road telephone exchange, then in its final stages of construction.

The 1960s

Once a great shipbuilding area, many fabulous ships were built and launched into the River Tees for over 120 years. But by the 1960s times were changing and fewer were being launched.

This decade was a time when there were still numerous vessels to be seen on the Tees, and here the giant Naess Parkgate is seen being launched in 1966.

I became a teenager in the 1960s, and at age 14 in 1966 (yes the year England won the Football World Cup, with some of the matches played in the town at Ayresome Park) I got my first camera. Thus my love of photography and especially of photographing the town's urban landscape began, with a particular fondness for my immediate vicinity and the town centre. I began chronicling the changes happening all around me, something I continue to do today.

In Middlesbrough even greater changes were happening that would fundamentally change the town forever. Wholesale redevelopment on an unprecedented scale swept away whole communities for impressive road schemes and new office and shopping developments. Row-upon-row of terraced houses were demolished in the Newport and Cannon Street areas, together with all the streets running off Union Street to Newport Road.

Huge building projects looked totally out of scale and occupied large areas of the once Victorian central core. The beautiful Hugh Bell Schools were demolished at the end of the 60s to be replaced by the current Magistrates Court, and streets were demolished in readiness for a new Civic Center on Russell Street. The United Reformed Church on Grange Road was demolished for the new Police Headquarters and the then Teesside Polytechnic began encroaching on its surroundings at the start of its expansion, which continues today but now as Teesside University.

By 1969/70 the retail revolution reached the town and the clearance of pubs, shops and streets of houses for the Cleveland Center began in the heart of the town. The Dundas Arcade, a forerunner built a few years earlier, was innovative and modern with a huge office buildings sitting directly above - a first for Middlesbrough.

Many Victorian schools were rebuilt, and other new schools built, including Easterside and Erith Grove (1961); St Mary's Sixth Form College and St Michael's RC Secondary and Captain Cook, Marton (1963), Nunthorpe Secondary and St Mary's Convent RC grammar school (1964), Kader School and St Edward's RC (1966), St Christopher's Joint RC/C of E, Holmwood on Saltersgill Avenue, Kirby College and Ormesby Secondary (1967). The frenzy of school building culminated with Netherfields (1968).

Many newly built churches made their appearance. They include the Free Baptist Church on Beverley Road and St Alphonusus Catholic Church, North Ormesby (1960), The Friends' Meeting House, Cambridge Road, St Margaret of Scotland, Brookfield, Nunthorpe Methodist Church (1961) Jehovah's Witnesses Kingdom Hall, St Bernadette's Catholic Church, Nunthorpe and the Muslim Mosque, Grange Road (1962), my Father being a founding member of the congregation. The Scandinavian Seamen's Mission on the corner of Linthorpe Road and Park Road South (1963), St Clare's Catholic Church, Brookfield (1965) and the original Sikh Temple at 6 Milton Street, along with St Agnes, Easterside (1967).

On the outskirts of the town the council continued apace with building estates such as Netherfields (1966), Overfields (1968) and the start of the vast new "town" at Hemlington (1969). All these Estates were built on greenfield sites thus pushing the town's boundaries southwards.

Readers may ask why I have not mentioned much about North Ormesby and they would be quite right. The reason is quite simple: very little in terms of change was taking place here in the first six decades of the 20th Century, other than the addition of three cinemas - the Gem (1910-1959), Pavillon (1911-1963) and the Majestic (1955-1974) - and minor shop alterations.

The only other major event in the North Ormesby area was the arrival of the trolley bus network in November 1919, only a few weeks before the start of our story in 1920. This system ran from the terminus of the tramways at North Ormesby Road to Grangetown via South Bank, giving the traveling public a comprehensive network from Norton all the way to Grangetown, passing additional routes at Middlesbrough Town Hall. However, in 1969 the extension of Borough Road via a new flyover finally ended the isolation of North Ormesby, linking it seamlessly with a sweeping viaduct from Smeaton Street to Borough Road East, thereby rendering the old railway crossing obsolete.

All was about to change for untouched and sleepy North Ormesby as the bulldozers of Middlesbrough Council set about more clearance, targeting the compact community. Vast swathes of the area's Victorian terraces were swept away and the central Market Place hub lost all the buildings on the north and west sides, plus the northern section of King's Road, leaving only the southern section.

The historic Anglo Saxon and European population of Middlesbrough was joined by new immigrants from the Commonwealth in the 60s. A small community of South Indians made Middlesbrough their home with the majority coming from the Mirpur District of Pakistani Kashmir. By the end of the decade single men were joined by their wives and children to form the basis of a thriving Asian community which became the largest in the Tees Valley.

In 1968 Middlesbrough joined the other towns of Stockton-on-Tees, Thornaby, Billingham, the Hartlepools, and Redcar to form the new County Borough Of Teesside, creating a large metropolitan Borough with a population exceeding 400,000.

Another ship launch and a stunning view of the once bustling shipbuilding industry near Middlesbrough.

Built in 1887, the surviving wall of the old Vulcan Street Salt Works, now Grade II listed, is shown here in the 1960s with the railway tracks still in place. It is a very rare survivor of the town's once vast industrial heritage.

Massive redevelopment took place in the late 1950s and 1960s in the old town located between the river and the railway line. It was a huge undertaking in order to clear slum houses and regenerate the area.

Much of the area was swept away culminating in the total destruction of the old town. Of the few prominent buildings to survive were the old town hall and Customs House. The old Market Hall is seen here being removed.

St. Hilda's church and the old Town Hall looking up East Street.

Also looking up East Street from roughly the same position, the new blocks of flats along Cleveland and Durham streets are complete, with one of the new blocks still under construction behind.

Durham Street is seen looking northwards towards the riverfront. The new flats are on the left with one block finished and another still under construction. Further along another block has yet to begin near the Captain Cook pub, seen at the end the street.

Durham Street leading from the railway station to the Transporter Bridge was a busy thoroughfare in the old town right up to the demise of the St. Hilda's area in the 1960's. The new flats did not last long, and today nothing remains of the scene above apart from the Transporter Bridge and Captain Cook pub.

Bolckow Street is now partially buried under the Hill Street Centre, as is the rest of the area around bounded by Hill Street, Wilson Street, Linthorpe Road and Newport Road.

Looking along towards Boundary Road, the three buildings beyond the Richards sign on the right still exist. The nearest on the right were demolished for a new Yorkshire Bank building, and those on the left are all under the shopping centre.

Another view looking down Bolckow Street towards St. Columba's Church. All of the buildings in this view other than the church itself have been demolished for the Hill Street Centre.

The notorious Cannon Street Riots of August 1961 were a significant political and public disorder event in Middlesbrough's young history. Following the death of a young white man in a fight with an Asian resident, hundreds of locals went to cause trouble outside the Taj Mahal Pakistani restaurant, where they met with a protective police barricade. Here in the photograph, the Taj Mahal is seen in the aftermath. It bore the brunt of the crowd's attention, but the crowd's attempt at burning it down succeeded only in breaking its windows. Numerous police officers were injured, and two are seen on patrol outside in this image some time after the riots on that hot August Saturday and Sunday.

A photograph showing the dilapidated state of Victorian houses in the Cannon Street area of town. Here in Eve Street looking down towards Granville Street, a lone lady stands in her doorway with her dog. The area's slum clearance programme was imminent and totally comprehensive.

Middlesbrough Railway Station in the mid 1960s without its once grand roof, which was bombed in 1942 and later demolished. The busy scene above shows a view of the platforms with people milling about. An unusual-looking train stands in the centre of the image.

Cannon Street was one of the most famous and well known in town. The community in and around it was one the originals in early Middlesbrough. In this image looking east towards Boundary Road, Cannon Street looks fairly deserted and devoid of life. By this time it was in decline.

Taken on 4th May 1966 by the council photographer, this is a rare view of Boundary Road looking down towards Cannon Street and St. Columba's Church. Everything else here has been demolished apart from the church, which remains marooned behind Sainsbury's, and the corner building on the right, which was until recently the Princess Alice pub.

Now buried under the Hill Street Centre, and typical of so many terraced streets now consigned to the history books, Vaughan Street can be seen here looking down towards Boundary Road.

Looking down Unthank Street towards one of the gas holders, with Mabel Street off to the right. Built in the late 1860s and 70s, it was a densely built-up working-class part of the town. The whole area has now been flattened but the gas holders still survive, and the area is now known as Cannon Park.

Millbank Street was a long row of terraced houses running from Newport Road to Marsh Road and crossing Cannon Street. These two amazing images taken in 1963 and 1964 show the street both before and after the residents moved out, with the second image detailing it in a derelict state ready for demolition.

Newport Road was the premier route out of town to Thornaby and Stockton. In these five views, the long lost heritage of this Middlesbrough road is shown. Nothing now remains except a few original buildings.

First, looking westwards in this 1965 photograph, is the County Hotel from 1866 seen on the corner of Lord Street. It was demolished in 1967 along with all the buildings seen here.

A fine view of Newport Road with the Acklam Hotel between the then Holt Street and Victoria Street. The faint outline of the old tram tracks is still visible on the road. All of the buildings in the image were swept away in the 60s and 70s apart from the Acklam Hotel, which survived until quite recently.

Newport Road at its western end close to the Tees (Newport) Bridge. The garage was a well known landmark close to the mini roundabout entrance to the bridge and St. Cuthbert's Church (now the Phoenix Center), which is the only building to survive in this view.

Looking back eastwards along Newport Road towards the town centre, and taken from a point close to the North Riding Infirmary out of shot on the right, the County and Palmerston public houses are on the left in the middle distance just past the Sparks sign. The Palmerston closed in 1966 and the County in 1967, being demolished soon after.

This view shows Newport Road busy with traffic and people. The picture is taken from outside the West End Methodist Chapel at Derwent Street on the right and Punch Street on the left.

This lovely view looking along Linthorpe Road shows Bottomley Street on the right. Taken on the 6th of the 6th, 1966, a somewhat unusual date, but quite apt as everything seen here on the right was demolished in 1969 in readiness for the building of the Cleveland Center.

Looking southwards along Linthorpe Road, and as in the previous picture all the buildings seen here were demolished for the construction of the Cleveland Centre.

The popular Victorian municipal swimming baths on Gilkes Street were demolished and the site was redeveloped into the Captain Cook Square shopping complex. This rare interior image of the main pool is still evocative and was little changed from its construction until its demise.

This very rare interior image from the early 1960s shows the cleaning staff busy in the main auditorium of the Odeon on Corporation Road. The Odeon was a very popular cinema in its time, with a Saturday kids club which many readers may recall. Children (like myself) were able to see several smaller shows plus one main feature, as well as enjoying a sing-along beforehand.

Looking eastwards along Corporation Road towards the Corporation Hotel and the Town Hall, with the newly rebuilt Binns store on the right showing its wares in large display windows. British Home Stores now occupies the site of the former "Big Wesley" chapel on the opposite corner.

A view westwards down Newport Road with Binns dominating the view (on the left), and a workman adding the new British Home Stores name to the exterior of the building.

These two amazing 1960s photographs show both Corporation Road and Albert Road. The Corporation Hotel dominates its corner site, and the once popular underground public lavatories are visible on the left.

Albert Road looking north towards the railway station. Both these remarkable photographs are of an era just within living memory for many, but are now viewed as historic images.

Dundas Arcade was completed in 1964 and is seen here almost finished. It was the town's first purpose-built shopping precinct, and the height of modernity. Hintons moved from their well known Corporation Road store into the shopping arcade in 1967 and ensured its success as they took ten units. The Dundas Arcade became an established shopping destination which continues to this day.

This truly fantastic series of photographs were taken from the top of Binns in 1961, looking from north to south across the town centre and east across the town towards North Ormesby.

The docks which are incredibly close to the town centre, and crammed full of ships.

The Town Hall and the Russell Street and Grange Road areas of the town in the background, with Russell Street running westwards ending at Marton Road and St. John's church tower, which is visible in the distance.

Looking across the Newton Street area (now occupied by the Cleveland Centre) towards the Hugh Bell schools and beyond. Sadly, other than a few landmarks such as the library and Constantine College, not much in this view has survived the destruction of these wonderful parts of the town.

Yet another magnificent aerial view of the town centre's long demolished buildings. Hugh Bell Schools (boys & girls) is seen in its entirety looking northwards across towards Victoria Square to the Town Hall and Transporter Bridge.

A magnificent aerial photograph taken in the late 1960s which has recorded the whole area now covered by the Cleveland Centre. The shopping centre opened in stages from August 1970 to 1973. Covering six acres and at the time containing 95 shops, a health centre, three pubs, offices and a rooftop car park, the centre is contained within the boundary of (starting top left) Corporation Road, Albert Road, Grange Road and Linthorpe Road.

Club Contessa located on Grange Road was a popular venue and very familiar to many young people in the swinging 60s. It is seen as its demolition was taking place.

The Trooper public house was once the only pub located on Waterloo Road, at the corner Wilton Street. The building still survives as a public house popular with students.

Two coloured postcards from the early 60s which I actually bought and kept from that time show scenes of the Victoria Square vicinity, where I used to visit on a daily basis.

The first shows my old school, Hugh Bell, which I attended from 1964 to 1968. The school is on the right opposite the police station. Also in this view is the Carnegie Public Library.

The second image is a marvellous view of the square looking towards the Town Hall, showing in colour the buildings on the left which were soon to be demolished for the Cleveland Centre. It also shows the houses behind the Town Hall which were demolished for the very ugly Civic Centre.

This incredible picture of a very smoky Grange Road area was taken from the top of the police station looking over Melrose Street and Jedburgh Street, looking eastwards towards Marton Road. Continued use of coal as a heating fuel and the close proximity of so many terraced houses meant this was a regular sight until smokeless zones came into operation in the 1970s.

Looking across Poplar Street towards Lennox Street, we see here the extent of the demolition taking place in the Russell Street and Grange Road area. Today this is the location of the entrance to MIMA from Centre Square.

The little Baptist Chapel which I used to pass on my way to school was situated at the corner of Pembroke Street and Grange Road. It was opened in 1891 but closed after 86 years in July 1977.

Taken on a wet day this interesting overview shows Borough Road with buildings now lost, including St. Richard's School on Woodlands Road behind the Gazette building, and the Friends Meeting House. Teesside House was built on the site of the latter, and has now been redeveloped as student accommodation.

An extremely rare image of the terrace of grand houses that once stood along Borough Road on the block next to the old Constantine College (now Teesside University), which can just be seen to the right. A great loss, these lovely old houses were torn down and replaced by a non-descript and ugly building, which itself was replaced by a modern university building.

The wonderfully Art Deco Regent Cinema on Parliament Road opened a year before the outbreak of World War II in 1938. The cinema was located outside of central Middlesbrough, making it very popular among the local population. But this did not save it from closure in 1961, and its subsequent demolition.

A never before published photograph of the row of substantial three storey houses that once stood on North Ormesby Road to the rear of St. John's Church. The Tees Valley Chinese Community Centre and its car park now occupy the site of these grand homes.

The flyover connecting Borough Road to Smeaton Street in North Ormesby is seen here under construction in 1969. It was a vital link which made it much easier to reach North Ormesby without needing to traverse the railway crossing, which could often lead to holdups.

Three views of North Ormesby show the area as it was in the late 1960s. First, a trolleybus is seen at the turnaround point at the bottom of Kings Road, for Southbank and Grangetown.

Holy Trinity Church of 1869 is seen here on market day. Today only the tower remains, with a newer church building alongside.

The Market Square full of traders and townsfolk selling and buying the goods on offer. Throughout the 60s this was our local market and twice a week I would accompany my mum and sister on what was a very exciting day out for me.

The Marton Hotel and Country Club as it was in its heyday in the 1960s, seen here from Marton Road as part of a series of Marton postcards. The hotel was burnt down in June 2019 and the site is now vacant awaiting a decision on its future.

Another Marton postcard shows the parade of shops built as the main retail area for this suburbs. They still exist, but additional shops are now provided by the indoor mall located in Coulby Newham.

These four photograps of Marton Hall show it as it was before and after the disastrous fire on 4th June 1960. The mansion was built in 1853 for the industrialist Henry Bolckow, who was also Middlesbrough's first MP, elected in 1868.

Marton Hall southern frontage before the fire.

The same frontage during the fire, with onlookers observing and firefighters in action.

The south frontage after the fire. The building, which was unoccupied at the time and already facing demolition, was deemed unstable and work was quickly brought about to clear it.

Men working to demolish the once lovely and elegant dome of the hall.

The 1970s

A lovely colour photograph taken in 1974 of the Teesside Magistrates Court looking up Albert Road towards the Town Hall. Opened officially in February 1973 on the site of my old secondary school, which had been on the south side of Victoria Square since 1892, the new court had a tunnel from it directly into the subterranean Middlesbrough Police Station across Dunning Street.

If the previous decade was the Swinging 60s, the new decade was being referred to as the Super 70s.

On TV at the time I recall a constant jingle that was playing with this theme. Indeed in Middlesbrough the 70s were a very special time as so much was to happen to change the town. The 60s were all about demolition and comprehensive redevelopment of the old Victorian town. The 70s became the decade that set the pace and continued delivering on these massive schemes.

This decade saw the opening of the Cleveland Centre, Middlesbrough's first large, modern indoor shopping Center, which was a sign of the town's progressive outlook and its ambition. Completed in stages, with the first section opening in 1971, it was and still is the largest of the town's four shopping centres, housing many major retailers. It has frontages on both Albert Road and Linthorpe Road, as well as entrances on Grange Road and Corporation Road, with rooftop car parking.

On the site of my old secondary school, Hugh Bell, a new combined court complex opened in 1971. The old Gaumont Cinema (formerly the Opera House) was demolished that year, despite showing its last film in 1961. A sad loss of another grand old building which was needlessly bulldozed in the name of progress.

The 70s was the decade in which a number of huge new office buildings made their appearance. In 1974 blocks including Gurney House, Church House and Corporation House (the tallest at 19 storeys) were completed, along with the Dragonara Hotel, the largest in the town. Towards the end of the 70s Vancouver House was built on Corporation Road.

There were fewer new schools built in the 1970s, but notable additions include Breckon Hill (1971), Allendale Road, Overfields (1972). In 1974 Abingdon Road school opened on the former convent site and the historic Acklam Hall was converted to become the new King's Manor complex which was previously Acklam High School.

New places of worship built in the 70s were St Andrew's United Reformed Church (1973), The Congregational Church, Union Street, Berwick Hills Salvation Army, and St Thomas More Catholic Church, Beechwood (1974), Ormesby Methodist Church (1975), Jamia Mosque Almadina, Waterloo Road (the former St Michael's Church) and the Salvation Army, Acklam (1976).

Housing development focussed in part on the St Hilda's area, redeveloping the historic town site with smaller projects such as Tower Green and along the north side of Union Street. But the bulk of the newer housing (both council and private) continued southwards in the ever expanding Hemlington and the beginnings of what would become Coulby Newham.

Roads infrastructure in and around Middlesbrough was also looking to the future in the 1970s, with the massive A19 Tees Viaduct opening in 1975, carrying the road northward into Durham, easing pressure on the Newport Bridge from the 1930s.

Durham Street looking north towards the river from its junction with Lower Feversham Street, with the newer 1960s council flats on the left now fully occupied. On the right are the older surviving Victorian terraced properties.

St Columba's Church, seen after the surrounding Cannon Street area had been demolished, looks quite marooned as it does today on the edge of the Sainsbury's car park. Opened on 20th March 1901 and now a Grade II listed building. It is a rare Victorian survivor in an area which was totally obliterated under the council's comprehensive slum clearances of the 1960s and 1970s.

A late 1970s photograph of Jordison & Co., then a well-known local printer, along with the old Masonic Hall located on Marton Road. This view is before the A66 cut through, flattening all in its path including all the buildings seen in this image.

Looking east down Wilson Street towards the Royal Exchange on the left. The A66 flyover has now sadly replaced all the buildings seen here except for the ones on the right.

The Albert Road frontage of the impressive Royal Exchange, looking south towards the Town Hall. The buildings beyond have survived the bulldozers, including the lovely turreted corner edifice currently the Chambers Bar and night club.

Taken from some height, this image looking east along Newport Road shows the mini roundabout at the junction of Hartington Road and Boundary Road. The recently closed Princess Alice pub is on the left, and all the buildings on the right were demolished for the new bus station.

The small but well used former United bus terminal at Newport Road. The view is approximately where the present Newport Road entrance to the newer Middlesbrough Bus Station is located.

Three very rare views of the Albert Road frontage of the Cleveland Centre under construction, which I photographed in 1971. I had been taking photos of the town since I was 14 and by age 19 had amassed quite a collection of the changing town.

This distinctive view shows the middle of the central section. The steelwork skeleton was to become the main office element of the development.

Taken at the same time, this image shows the first office block section of the Cleveland Centre complete and occupied, facing Albert Road. This block stands on what was once the entrance to Newton Street, and presently the site of the restaurant Bistrot Pierre.

Further along are the remaining block of buildings that were spared when the Cleveland Centre was built. However, they were not to survive long with all except the three-storey brick office block being demolished for the giant 19-floor Corporation House, which was completed in 1974. Now Centre North East and still is the tallest office building in Middlesbrough and the Tees Valley.

An interesting view looking along Dunning Street in the direction of Borough Road with Victoria Square seen here on the right. Taken in mid-1972 as the Magistrates Court is in the final stages of construction. The court was not officially opened until 2nd February 1973. Teesside House and the then Teesside Polytechnic Tower can be seen beyond dominating Borough Road. In the photograph the lovely terrace of houses adjoining the central library are still standing. Today where they once stood is part of the new layout of Centre Square leading to the MIMA gallery.

A wintry image looking across the then Poplar Street towards Grange Road taken in 1971. It is a terrific view taken from the Town Hall, showing what is now the site of the MIMA art gallery and the Town Lake. The scene depicted shows the total and comprehensive scale of the destruction of the Victorian townscape of the last 50 years that has changed on an epic scale.

A truly amazing aerial photograph of the whole of the town centre looking northwards over the central terraced housing areas, of which nothing remains today except the few houses bounded by Abingdon Road, Grange Road, Marton Road and Borough Road. Taken in 1971, the ground has been cleared ready for the new Magistrates Court and new Marton House is under construction at the bottom left, both not completed till 1973.

Another incredibly detailed aerial photograph of the town centre looking northwards in the direction of the river. At bottom right is Marton House and one of the large Victorian houses that once stood next to it, now both demolished for the Newlands Medical Centre. The core and lift shaft can be seen as construction begins on Corporation House opposite the Town Hall, which was completed in 1974.

Vast swathes of the town were cleared in the late 1960s and 70s in readiness for the construction of the A66 from its new eastern link to North Ormesby and beyond. Seen here in the marvellous aerial view is the Newport area around the approach road to Newport Bridge. The Newport Library and flats, plus St. Cuthbert's Church are visible and the truncated terraced streets which still stand. At bottom left can be seen the Newport Schools on Victoria Street, which were opened in 1885 and closed in 1978.

Another high vantage image this time taken from Gurney House in the late 70s looking to where the A66 viaduct now is. At bottom right the wall that can be seen is still in place. It was once the rear boundary of the Dragonara Hotel's service area and currently serves the same function for the Jurys Inn.

A fantastic aerial view of the town centre taken in early 1972. On closer inspection the final stages of the Cleveland Centre are still under construction, which was not completed and officially opened till 1973. On the left, the new Clarendon Building at Teesside Polytechnic is under construction.

This view from the roof of the Gazette building shows the Transporter Bridge, Rede House and the roof tops of Russell Street and Corporation Road. The church steeple is the Unitarian Church which stood on Corporation Road opposite Gurney Street. The church and buildings to its right are now the Combined Crown Court.

This nostalgic image is looking along Albert Road north towards the Railway Station. Although only superficial changes have occurred, the lovely red double decker United bus on its way to West Hartlepool brings back many memories of the era.

This view of St. George's United Reformed Church on the corner of Princes Road and Linthorpe Road, which was opened on 23rd October 1894 and closed for services on 29th May 1966, lasting only a little over 62 years. It was not demolished until the 1980s. The row of shops beyond and adjoining the church were known as the Green Shops due to the colour of their glass display windows. Now the site of a care home and student flats known as Linthorpe Hall 248, which I consider to be one of the ugliest buildings ever constructed in the town especially on such a high profile site.

Taken on one of my old cameras, these two images show the row of buildings that were lost to the bulldozers in the early 1970s. The first looks west along Corporation Road. The Odeon can just be glimpsed at the end of the row of buildings. These 1860s houses made way for the present James Cook House, which opened in 1997, and the new road linking Corporation Road to Wilson Street, Marton Road and the A66.

The second image looks back eastwards from the corner of the Odeon, which can be seen on the left.

This trio of buildings are remarkable in their survival from the onslaught of 21st Century redevelopment in the town centre. Although little has changed I have included them as they are the only Victorian buildings other than the corner pub to still be standing on this part of Corporation Road east of the Town Hall and old Empire music hall. The building nearest the camera currently houses the Multi Media Exchange, La Pharmacie restaurant and the Medicine Bar. It was temporarily the premises of Binns when their original building was destroyed by fire, and later acted as a warehouse for the store.

A stunning night-time photograph showing the then Corporation House with its lights blazing, looming over the Town Hall clock. In the foreground construction is underway on Vancouver House on Gurney Street.

Severn Street, seen here looking towards Borough Road, was the archetypical Middlesbrough Victorian terraced street. As can be seen in the image, it even had a corner shop.

Wye Street also in the Rivers area looking towards Borough Road. The Middlesbrough telephone exchange building can be seen looming at the end of the street.

Taken some time in 1978 from the top of Corporation House (now Centre North East) this coloured photograph is looking over the construction site of Vancouver House, towards Marton Road and Middlesbrough Dock. As yet there is no A66 Viaduct, and the housing complex has not begun construction where the cars are parked outside Gurney House. This and the Dragonara Hotel can be clearly seen, looking quite new having only been completed a few years earlier.

Vancouver House seen here just prior to its opening in 1979, with hoardings still around the Corporation Road entrances. Vancouver House, which housed a public house, shops and five floors of offices, has been used by various administrative departments of Middlesbrough Council. Currently there is planning permission in place for the building to have two extra floors added and conversion to a hotel.

Taken in 1975, here I am leaning over the railing talking one cousin while another is taking the photograph. Seen here in a wasteland of cleared houses that once stood in Grange Road, the image is looking across to Russell Street and the new Civic Centre. The Town Hall can be seen behind the houses on Gloucester Street. The area is now covered by the MIMA art gallery and Town Lake.

Russell Street is seen in this image from around 1974 with the northern side already demolished and the southern awaiting its fate. The new Middlesbrough Registry Office which was opened in Aril 1973 can just be seen on the right at the end of the Russell Street.

Taken looking westwards along Grange Road from close to Lennox Street, near where my family lived just out of camera shot. In the distance is Church House under construction, reaching almost to its full height of 15 floors. The little Methodist church on the corner of Pembroke Street is awaiting demolition and other houses along the road are internally stripped ready to be cleared.

A block of Victorian houses which are very important in my life as it was here at 185 Grange Road that I was born on 27th October 1952. Seen here in 1977, 185 is the second house in from the right, where the couple are passing. The houses here on the corner of Abingdon Road (on the right) and Grange Road were just over a hundred years old when the photograph was taken.

Opened in March 1876, these images show St. Johns Church of England School on Bright Street just after its closure in 1971. Subsequently demolished, the Ironopolis social club now occupies the site.

In the first picture, looking towards Grange Road, our shop is just visible. This is where we moved as a family in 1962. The second picture is a view of the school looking towards Russell Street. The stone pillar that can be seen on the extreme right unbelievably still stands at the entrance to the small public car park on Bright Street, as do the first two houses at the end far end of the image.

The stone pillar that can be seen in the previous image can be seen here on the extreme left. This grand house once stood proudly on the corner of Bright Street and Grange Road and was for a time used by the Territorial Army with the adjoining Drill Hall. The process of demolition has begun, but I believe I have managed to capture the essence of its Victorian architecture. It was a popular landmark on this part of the road and stood opposite the house that I was brought up in. The old drill hall survives and is used as the Middlesbrough Youth Training Centre. The rest of the site is a car park.

A wonderful view looking westwards down Borough Road from the corner of Abingdon Road in the early 1970s. The image shows all the terraces of large Victorian houses that once lined this road, many of which have now been demolished or turned into commercial premises. This particular procession is passing Melrose Street which ran off Borough Road to Grange Road and is now the site of Melrose House which stands ready for demolition.

Not the prettiest of buildings, the well-known pawnbrokers of Greenwoods seen here on its North Ormesby Road site prior to its demolition. Greenwoods were known to generations of Middlesbrough folk who used its services regularly. Now long gone it once stood near to the railway crossing, the track is still visible here, however, it is now buried under the A66 dual carriageway.

Ayresome Park football ground was opened in 1903 but was sadly demolished in 1997. One of its four stands is seen here in the 1970s. With a capacity of over 26,600, it was the second home of Middlesbrough Football Club, who moved to the Riverside Stadium in 1995. The ground famously hosted three games in the 1966 World Cup, with the North Koreans playing all their matches at Ayresome Park.

A late 70s view of Newport Road from the then Corporation House looking towards the Newport and Cannon Street areas which have now been cleared of housing. The construction works in progress seen beyond St. Columbas Church on the top right are for the A66 dual carriageway and elevated roundabout. In the foreground are the upper levels of Binns and Newhouses.

Nazareth House seen here from Park Road North was the Middlesbrough orphanage and care home for the destitute. Established in 1880, the Victorian building was part of a larger complex, much of which still stands. Nazareth House was later demolished and replaced by the present care home.

From 1969 to 1972 I attended Kirby College (previously Kirby School) on Roman Road. The college is seen here with the original school buildings on the left behind the tall chimney, and the newer education blocks on the centre and right of the photograph. All the buildings have now been replaced with an up-market housing complex.

St. Margaret's Church on The Oval is seen here from the eastern side in the early 1970s. Opened on 12th May 1961, this church serves the Brookfield suburb on the southern edge of Middlesbrough. The little wooden church hall on the left of the main church is now long gone, replaced by a modern hall complex serving the surrounding community.

The 1980s

Victoria Square as it was, before the changes that were to come. This layout was the second in the square's history. First, after its initial opening in 1901, it had a bandstand in the centre and paths leading directly into the middle. Three of the town's public buildings, the Central Library, Police Station (now demolished) and the Magistrates Court can be seen surrounding the square.

In the 1980s Middlesbrough saw the completion of the majority of its massive road infrastructure projects which would almost encircle the town, with the A19 and A66 to the west, north and east, and the A174 Parkway to the south.

As a result, the early part of the decade saw many buildings in the town centre demolished to make way for the A66 trunk road which was built to link east and west. The elevated roadway meant the loss of the iconic Victorian Royal Exchange, plus buildings in Newport, and along Wilson Street.

Housing at Coulby Newham continued to expand and the Parkway Shopping Center opened in 1986 to serve the new communities being established to the south of the town. Infill private estates also continued being built at Marton along Ladgate Lane and in Nunthorpe, Ormesby and Acklam.

Large new commercial projects emerged, such as the Hill Street Center which opened in late 1981, as well as the new Bus Station in 1982. Pat Phoenix (Elsie Tanner of Coronation Street fame) came to open the new Bus Station in a blaze of publicity. Both of these developments emerged as the result of the clearance of scores of terraced streets where once tightly knit communities and small businesses stood. Only older residents will recall the streets and shops that were at the time so well known.

The Russel Street and Grange Road area was comprehensively cleared to make way for the promised relocation from London of the PSA government department which was to be housed in a complex of office buildings. Grange Road was realigned from Victoria Square to Abingdon Road for this purpose, but the PSA never arrived and a whole community was wantonly destroyed. Among the casualties was our family home at 185 Grange Road and all the familiar streets and local landmarks of my youth.

In their place social housing was eventually built with former street names being the only link to the area's heritage as Elder, Hazel and Rutland courts emerged from the rubble of a whole community consigned to history in one fell swoop. At the other end of Grange Road on the former Monkland Street to Borough Road another area of old Victorian terraced streets was demolished to make way for more social housing which was erected in the 80s.

Macmillan City Technology College opened its doors to an eager populous in the 80s. It was one of the first of its kind in the country, being a flagship project of the Government's educational programme. Many of my family have graced its doors including my two nephews, Harroon Chohan (who sadly passed away aged only 17) and Khurram Chohan who now lives and works in California.

Places of worship that were opened in the 1980s include the replacement for the old St Mary's Catholic Cathedral "Over The Border" in St Hilda's. The new Cathedral on Dalby Way in Coulby Newham was consecrated by Archbishop Cardinal Basil Hume on 15th May 1988. Other new places of worship for the Muslim community saw two mosques opening - the Zia Ul Quran on Bow Street (1982) in the former St Alban's Church, and the Abu Bakr, on Park Road North (1989).

This interesting aerial view of the town is looking towards the empty docks. The Royal Exchange can be seen at the extreme left, with buildings to its east having been cleared on the line of the soon-to-be-built A66 extension. Corporation Road, Russell Street and Grange Road are all seen running across the image, with only the buildings along Corporation Road still standing. The streets where hundreds of terraced houses once stood have all been cleared and the area awaits the developments of the 80s and 90s. Here the Town Lake, Combined Courts and various office buildings and modern housing would soon be built.

Although not an aerial photograph, this view looking up Grange Road West has been taken 15 floors up in Church House. It looks down upon an area of town that is ready for the developments to come. On the left of Grange Road is the cleared Monkland Street area (now the Westward/Monkland Court housing estate). To the right the area is now covered by the Captain Cook Square shopping complex and multi-storey car park. On the right is the lovely Tower House (now McDonald's), a truly sad loss of one of the towns best looking buildings.

The new A66 trunk road linking Stockton, Darlington and the A19 with Middlesbrough and East Cleveland was a major construction event of the 1980s. In Middlesbrough the new road meant a huge clearance and construction programme where a massive viaduct was built cutting through the town centre. The series of images that follow show buildings lost and various construction stages of the project.

These buildings on Wilson Street which survived the World War II bombing were the first to be demolished.

Further along Wilson Street on Albert Road was the Royal Exchange, which was one of the premier buildings of the Victorian era and, other than the Town Hall, was the grandest and largest of them all. Opened in 1868 it succumbed like so many fine buildings to the onslaught of the A66. Shown here from Marton Road where the bus station once stood, it met its fate in 1985 when it was demolished in readiness for the new road.

A view of Severn Street looking north towards North Ormesby Road.

The Rivers streets seen from the top of Marton House before they were demolished.

The beautiful and very opulent Star and Garter Hotel standing on Marton Road prior to its demolition. The hotel lay directly in the path of the new viaduct, as did the many houses, small businesses and office buildings along this section of Marton Road which have already been cleared in readiness for the new A66.

Although this part of Marton Road was mainly housing, there were small business premises which also succumbed to the bulldozers for the A66.

These two photographs show the new A66 viaduct at the height of construction in 1986. In the first, the proximity to the railway station is evident.

The second picture is a wider view of the construction on roughly the same site that the Royal Exchange once stood. It shows how close the viaduct is to the remaining buildings around the area that survive to this day.

Church House seen here from Victoria Square in the mid-1980s looks very pristine in comparison with how it looks today. Built in the 1970s and empty for much of its existence, the building has planning consent to be converted into flats. However, regarded as an eyesore, as yet no movement on its refurbishment has occurred and it stands forlorn dominating this part of the town centre.

Looking east down Corporation Road, showing the original Rede House office block and Odeon cinema. Further along all the buildings have been demolished and the Odeon building will follow in 2006. Still named Rede House, the office block has been given a completely new façade and is now student flats.

All the buildings along Russell Street, as well as the streets running off it, were demolished by the late 1970s and in their place many new buildings were later constructed. However, the line of the original street is still in evidence being almost completely pedestrianized and renamed The Boulevard.

Here looking eastwards towards St. John's Church on Marton Road at the very start of the 1980s, the Hazel Court housing development can be seen under construction in the distance.

Hazel Court seen here in the later stages of construction was one two planned housing developments (the other being Elder Court) on the cleared streets bounded by Russell Street and Grange Road.

Fountain Court is a three storey office block fronting Grange Road at its junction with Melrose Street. It is seen here under construction in 1989. At the rear of the building there is private parking for up to 50 cars.

An unusual view looking from the junction of Corporation Road on the left and Marton Road on the right. It shows the then Borough Hotel public house, currently known as Dr Browns, after three other name changes. Gurney House and the Royal Exchange can be seen in the background. Today James Cook House obscures the view and the end of Corporation Road is blocked off. The Cineworld cinema complex now occupies the site on the right.

Grange Road looking west from Somerset Street. Once it was one of the grandest of Middlesbrough thoroughfares and was lined with large three storey Victorian Houses. All that remains today are two blocks of five houses. The block behind the tree is personal to me as it has contained our family home and corner shop since 1962.

Looking down towards Grange Road East, all the houses seen in the image have been demolished except for the corner building seen on the left, which was once the garage of Pallister, Yare & Cobb. The St. John's housing estate now covers the area on the right hand side of the road.

All the building visible in the image (other than the large former Baptist church building to the left) were demolished, to be occupied by the A66, new cinema and restaurant complex.

All the houses in this view and the street layout have all gone and are now covered by the small modern development currently comprising of Pizza Hut, McDonald's, Subway, American Golf, and the Hardware Supply Co. plus a large car park.

Taken from the Borough Road flyover to North Ormesby, the view here is looking towards the town centre with the now truncated North Ormesby Road in the foreground. The once prominent Greenwoods pawnbrokers and its large three storey building can be seen centre right. St. John's church tower and Corporation House are clearly visible on the skyline.

The five storey Marton House office building on Borough Road. Now demolished and replaced by the Newlands Medical Centre and pharmacy, this was a well-built brick building but lay vacant for many years before it succumbed to the bulldozers.

Marton Road Schools was for generations a well-known local landmark in this part of Middlesbrough. Opening in 1898, the school finally closed in March 1980 but was not completely demolished until 2001. Seen here in the late 1980s the site is still not built upon, but plans for an either an apartment block or a student block have been approved.

Viewed from the roof of now the demolished Marton House and looking westwards along Borough Road, the image shows several blocks of houses that have been demolished and replaced with newer buildings as well as the area behind where Elder Court, the town lake and MIMA now stand.

Taken at the same time as the previous image from the roof of Marton House, I turned the camera around to take this image of Marton Road Schools. Following closure the school buildings were used by the council for various purposes such as storage, until they were no longer needed.

A view of the main stand at Ayresome Park football ground in the late 1980s with a game in full play. Now demolished, a new housing development sprang up soon after the "Boro" had moved to the Riverside Stadium in 1995.

Middlesbrough General was the town's main hospital and had been amalgamated with Holgate Hospital in 1943. However, the new South Tees Hospital, now known as James Cook University Hospital, consolidated all the old hospitals on one site and eventually the old buildings were demolished in 2003. The image shows the wing that faced onto Roman Road. A housing development now covers the whole of the former hospital site.

Situated on the corner of Roman Road and St. Barnabas Road the building shown here was once the lodge house for the former Holgate part of the hospital. It has now been replaced by a block of flats.

Once part of the Prissick Educational Campus, with a collection of schools such as Brackenhoe, Brookside and Bertram Ramsay, Middlesbrough College on its Marton Road campus is seen before it and all the other schools moved to the new Middlehaven site. All are now history.

Acklam High School, later Acklam Sixth Form College, merged with Kirby College to form Middlesbrough College in 1995 but is seen here in the 1980s in its Hall Drive setting. Restored and now used as a restaurant and wedding venue, the Hall is Middlesbrough's only Grade I listed building.

The 1990s

This wonderful aerial image taken in the mid-1990s shows all of the newer and more modern buildings constructed since the 1980s. A very clear view of the Town Lake, Central Gardens, Combined Courts complex and the other office blocks can be seen fronting The Boulevard (what was once Russell Street). South of the lake is Fountain Court and Melrose House on Grange Road, plus the new housing of Hazel Court and Elder Court to the east, at the top of the photograph.

This was the decade in which many of the older buildings in the town were overhauled and given a makeover, or even a completely new look to bring them up to date. The Cleveland Centre lost its original white tile look and emerged with new frontages along Linthorpe Road and Albert Road. Some of the older office blocks were now deemed outdated and lay empty, but as in previous decades there were plenty of new construction projects which were changing the town's overall appearance.

One of the largest of these was the new Captain Cook Square open-air shopping centre built adjacent to the Bus Station and on the site of the old Gilkes Street Swimming Baths. The centre was opened by the then Middlesbrough Football Clubmanager Bryan Robson in 1999.

Other major building projects of the 90s included the Combined Crown Court complex opened in April 1992. It is next to the lovely town lake between Russel Street and Grange Road which was completed in 1990. The Bottle of Notes sculpture, which incorporates words from Captain James Cook's journal, was also erected here in 1993. Designed by internationally famous sculptor Claes Oldenburg and his wife Coosje Van Brugge, it is his only work in the UK to this date.

More office buildings were built in the decade including the Cleveland Business Center on Russell Street and Fountains Court on Grange Road, both in 1990. These were followed by Middlesbrough House on Corporation Road in 1991 and 100, Russell Street in 1992 housing the Inland Revenue. James Cook House opened in 1997 on Corporation Road.

A major event of the 1990s was the construction and relocation of the town's football stadium. With the historic Ayresome Park now outdated and limited in capacity, a brand new site was found alongside the old Middlesbrough Dock to the east of the town centre. On 26th August 1995 the Riverside Stadium opened as the new home of Middlesbrough Football Club.

Teesside Polytechnic became Teesside University in 1992 and began a phase of developing its town centre campus, starting with an impressive new library in 1997. Expansion continues to this day with millions of pounds of investment seeing the facility become a major UK educational institution.

New places of worship in the 1990s include the Church of the Transfiguration on Penistone Road, the Salvation Army's new premises in Pallister Park, and the Church of the Ascension of Christ in Penrith Road. Anew mosque was converted from the old Central Methodist Church on Southfield Road in 1998. On the educational front one major institution was formed when the old Kirby College and Acklam Sixth Form College merged in August 1995 to form Middlesbrough College.

A daytime view looking upstream towards what was the Ironmasters District, framed by the Transporter Bridge. The gondola is in mid-crossing on its way from the Yorkshire side at St. Hilda's to the Durham side at Port Clarence.

The Captain Cook public house can be seen here from across Durham Street. What was once a very popular drinking establishment in the town is now empty and waiting for someone to rescue and develop it for any use, and thereby saving it for posterity.

The Dock Tower prior to restoration seen here in splendid isolation, but still an imposing dockland landmark which fortunately has survived to the present day. Much of this area remained derelict through the 1990s. The new Snow Centre is planned to join the tower if the present plans come to fruition.

This lovely image taken in the now empty Middlesbrough Dock shows the 64-year-old Ukrainian vessel Tovarisch berthed for an intended restoration in 1997.

This 1990s view of the Middlesbrough Dock area was taken from Gurney House. The Dock is shown empty and devoid of any developments, with the small blue bridge over the dock entrance open presumably to allow a ship to pass through, although none is in sight. At this stage there is no Riverside Stadium, Middlesbrough College or any other developments as they are all yet to be built.

A view of St Mary's Cathedral on Sussex Street in the late 1990s as seen from Middlesbrough Railway Station's platform. Only a few years later the Cathedral was to burn to the ground, with the town losing an iconic Victorian building to add to the many that had gone before.

The Riverside Stadium which replaced Ayresome Park as the home of Middlesbrough Football Club is seen here nearing its completion in 1995. The new 30,000 all-seated stadium was constructed by the firm of Taylor Woodrow for £16 million, in only around nine months. Then standing alone, it has been joined by other Middlehaven projects giving the area a more built-up feel.

The Riverside Stadium's main entrance, photographed during a "golden sunlight" evening.

Queen's Terrace was one of the premier terraces of houses that were constructed in the old town, and remained so until the area's decline from the 1950s onwards. Built around 1840, this very dignified row of eight private houses are Grade II listed, and thus have survived the wrecking ball which has decimated most of the buildings in the old original town north of the railway line. The photograph was taken by me in early 1998 soon after the solicitor's firm of Jackson, Monk & Rowe moved out in December 1997. Although boarded up for many years they have now been restored to their former glory.

Overlooking Corporation Road towards the Eston Hills, this clear photograph shows the proximity of the countryside to the south of the town. St. John's Church dominates the view with its tower looming over Marton Road. Taken from Gurney House before James Cook House was built, it shows the listed trio of restored Victorian buildings on Corporation Road, and the Malt Shovel pub (now Dr. Browns).

The demolition of the once popular Gilkes Street public swimming baths enabled the council to construct a new shopping complex on the site, together with nearby cleared land, known as Captain Cook Square. The three images here depict the new shopping centre under construction in early 1998

The main entrance to the centre from Glikes Street with the steelwork well advanced ready for the official opening on 27th October 1999. This date was Captain James Cook's 271st birthday, and also coincidentally just happened to be my 47th birthday. I was present at the ceremony but only as a bystander!

The steelwork is complete and is ready for the brickwork to commence at the main entry point from Gilkes Street. A small row of Victorian shops was demolished, as well as an open-air car park.

Looking in the opposite direction eastwards towards Linthorpe Road, with the Brentnall Car Park on the left.

I often had friends walk around town with me on my photographic expeditions so that they could take a photograph with me in it just for fun. Here I am walking past the shutter carrying a large wallet on Glikes Street, past the old houses which were demolished soon after, and the rear of the old Woolworths building to my right. The replacement building on this corner is currently a Greggs bakery.

Glikes Street shops as they were before the changes of the late 1990s. With only one block on the right surviving, the redevelopment that became the Captain Cook Square shopping centre now takes up most of this space.

The Gilkes Street municipal swimming baths were the only ones in the town centre and since their opening in 1884 were well used and very popular. Demolished in the 1990's they were replaced by the open air Captain Cook Shopping Complex.

Looking down Gilkes Street with the façade of the swimming baths.

A closer view of the corner of the baths looking down Gilkes Street towards Middlesbrough Bus Station.

Taken from the top floor of Church House this view looks over Linthorpe Road towards Hartington Road and Union Street. The housing complex that can be seen under construction is on the area once occupied by the Monkland, Westward, Birks and Head streets community.

Also taken from Church House at the very beginning of 1990, this view is looking eastwards along Grange Road to North Ormesby and the Eston Hills beyond.

The Albert Road frontage but this time looking northwards towards the Town Hall with Victoria Square on the right. The old tiled façade was quite popular and much liked so there was sadness on the removal and upgrading of the building before the new hotel was planned.

Looking along Corporation Road towards its junction with Marton Road, Rede House is on the left. The Odeon Cinema is still standing in the background.

The very imposing new Combined Court Centre complex seen here with hoarding still around The Boulevard entrance, nearing completion in late 1990. Brought into use on 13th May 1991, it was not officially opened until 10th April the following year.

The New Town Lake with its ornamental spouting fountain and waterfall surrounded by Central Gardens, officially opened on 7th May 1989 but are seen here in an image taken sometime in late 1990s as the hoardings still surround the Combined Court at the extreme right of the picture.

Teesside House, fronting Borough Road, was a well-known 1970s office building which has always dominated its vicinity. Now a Teesside University student accommodation building, its exterior is largely unrecognizable from its original design, seen in this image, with an additional block now attached to the original building.

Once the Midland Bank and then, for many years, Bridgfords estate agency. This building on the corner of Linthorpe and Borough roads is currently a Greek Taverna. It is a lovely Edwardian survivor of the demolitions of the town's heritage by the planners.

Middlesbrough General Hospital had an entrance for pedestrians only on Ayresome Street, and for vehicles on Roman Road. Seen in this image is the latter with the Victorian buildings of this now-lost facility all present. The entire hospital site is now a modern housing development.

One of the many grand Victorian mansions that graced the Marton Road and Belle Vue areas of the town. This lovely old house named Brynteg once stood on Bell Vue Grove and was built in 1878. The date of the photograph was 6th June 1995, showing the house some nine months before its demolition in March 1996. Now long gone like so many of Middlesbrough's grand old houses. The site now has a care home built upon it.

The 2000s

The new Middlesbrough Institute of Modern Art (MIMA) gallery seen in its final stages of construction. Other landmarks can be seen beyond the Town Lake such as the Civic Centre and the Town Hall, as well as the old Registry Office building which was demolished in 2018. For many years this area was the site of row upon row of terraced houses. They were all cleared to make way for this open space in the heart of the town centre.

Starting the new millennium off with a bang, in 2001 the modern UGC multiplex cinema (which later became Cineworld) consisting of 11 screens, plus restaurant and retail outlets, opened alongside the A66 and Marton Road. This came at the cost of the older, smaller cinemas in the town – the last of which was the Odeon on Corporation Road, which was demolished in 2006 after operating as a nightclub for five years.

Teesside University continued its expansion through the acquisition of older buildings that surrounded the original polytechnic site in the heart of the town, centred around the 1930s Constantine Building and the 1960s Tower Block. The 2000s saw a surge in new buildings, with the Virtual Reality Centre, the Center for Enterprise, the Phoenix, Athena and Centuria South all opening.

Middlesbrough College continued its growth by merging with Teesside Tertiary College in 2002 and then moved to a state-of-the-art £80 million building next to the old Middlesbrough Dock in 2007.

Another new educational institution in this decade was the Unity City Academy on Ormesby Road, which opened in 2002. Coulby Newham came of age with its own King's Academy at Marton Farm opening September 2003.

On 27th January 2007 an exciting new ultra-modern building opened to the public. The Middlesbrough Institute of Modern Art, or MIMA, was the first purpose-built modern art gallery in the town's history, and the only one since the closure of the former art gallery on Linthorpe Road which had served the town since 1957. Other art venues were the Cleveland Craft Center which closed in January 2003 and its sister venue, the Cleveland Gallery which closed in 1999. All their collections were now housed under one roof at MIMA.

At the same time the old Victoria Square at the heart of the town was transformed from its 20th Century layout into a much larger area with the unimaginative name of Centre Square. The statues of John Vaughan and Sir Samuel Sadler were moved from their original positions which had them facing each other across the square. New fountains alongside the Town Hall are now popular, and the new layout gives the town a huge expansive space for public events which is second to none. Middlesbrough had come of age and had shrugged off its old "Smoggy" image as a modern post-industrial town as progressive and cosmopolitan as any in the country.

Launched in 2007, the impressive plans for the former Middlesbrough Dock were a media sensation and had the vision of an ultra-modern dockside community featuring office and residential buildings. The area was renamed Middlehaven and was a serious plan at the time, but ultimately became a pipe dream with few of the planned structures emerging. The publicity was expansive and visually stunning brochures produced for public consumption.

Industrial buildings such as these were all swept away for the new Mddlehaven plan. Now redeveloped for the first of these plans to come to fruition, this part of the former St. Hilda's area is now occupied by the new Middlesbrough College and other buildings.

A familiar sight from the 1960s onwards, Zetland House finally faced the axe shortly after this photograph was taken. Originally envisaged as a modern answer to a lack of office space in the area, it became an eyesore which blighted the history of Middlesbrough Station which it sat above. It was demolished in 2006.

This former Methodist church opened on Corporation Road in 1883. In 1926 it became the Cleveland Scientific Institute and remained so till the mid-21st Century. It was sadly demolished overnight before it could be listed in 2006. Many considered it a beautiful example of Middlesbrough's ecclesiastical history.

Originally a UGC cinema, later becoming a Cineworld, the 11 screen complex is one of the largest such venues in the Tees Valley. It is seen under construction in the early 2000s.

The brand-new multi-screen cinema complex nearing completion at what is now known as St John's Gate. It opened as the UGC Cinema in June 2001 but has since been rebranded as a Cineworld. The overall complex now includes a gym and several restaurants.

Viewed from roughly the same position as the first picture, the completed cinema complex dominates the mini roundabout at its junction with Marton Road and Wilson Street.

The North Riding Infirmary which was closed in 2003 and stood empty for some time as attempts to save it failed. However, after four years of public outcry, the bulldozers finally moved in and the iconic Newport Road building was demolished. A Travelodge hotel and Aldi supermarket now stand on the site.

The Bottle of Notes sculpture outside MIMA fronting the present Centre Square and Town Lake.

This corner Building is reflective of the architecture of the Captain Cook Square Shopping precinct. Covering the area once occupied by residential streets and the old Gilkes Street swimming baths, this corner is on Park Street and is viewed from Newport Crescent.

A row of mixed retail and residential terraces on Borough Road including an outlet of Jack Hatfield Sports. In the background the dome of The Crown is visible. These buildings date from the late 1800s, built where formerly open fields stretched towards Linthorpe.

Olympic medal winner Jack Hatfield is one of Middlesbrough's most famous sons. He lived from 1893 to 1965, and following his sporting career in swimming and water polo, he set up his Jack Hatfield Sports business. It soon moved to this Borough Road location, which was still going strong in the 2000s.

Middlesbrough Council's plans for the Gresham area of the town centre were originally to see a comprehensive redevelopment initiated by the then Mayor Ray Mallon. The plans were later scaled back and now refurbishment of some of the houses is under way, with a student village planned where once fine Victorian streets and houses stood. The photographs here were taken during on one of my many photographic town walkabouts in 2008.

Amber Street looking towards the rear of The Crown and Borough Road in the final few years before its terraced houses were demolished to make way for a new student housing development.

The ornate brick arrangement on the nearest terrace in Emerald Street indicates the year of construction as 1887 - a time when Middlesbrough was advancing south rapidly due to the influx of workers arriving in the town.

This unusual shaped house on the corner of Coral Street and Diamond Road in Gresham was a rare survivor, but by the late 2000s it had been boarded up, along with its neighbours, as one of the blocks earmarked for demolition.

The Boro Chippy on the corner of Garnet Street and Diamond Road is seen in the late 2000s and very proudly displaying its affection for Middlesbrough FC.

Located behind St. Cuthbert's Church off West Lane, a small area of terraced streets formed a tight knit community that was demolished wholesale in a comprehensive redevelopment in the early years of the new millennium.

Tarran Street is seen here from West Lane in 2002. It was replaced by more modern, but not actually much bigger, homes. Extras advertised in the new development included car parking spaces and greenery.

Cunningham Street seen here had slightly larger houses with bay windows. These were homes, not just houses, and a long standing community was uprooted and dispersed in the name of progress.

Vancouver House on its Gurney Street corner site makes an imposing statement in the town centre. Since its opening in 1979 the building has been in use as local government offices, with retail units on the Corporation Road frontage.

Rede House, originally clad in pre-stressed concrete panels, was completed in August 1970. It was modernised with a brand new façade and now houses ground floor retail units with student flats above.

The Gables on Marton Road was once a grand Grove Hill mansion which became a health clinic as far back as 1947. It was well used, but burnt down and the site sold in 2006. Subsequently two blocks of flats were built upon the site.

Fountain court here viewed from the Town Lake. It is one of the more successful of the town centre office buildings, having been continually occupied from its opening in the early 1990s.

The 2010s

The Captain Cook pub stands derelict awaiting a better future.

The ten years from 2010 to 2020 have seen a flood of schemes aimed at regenerating Middlesbrough's town centre, and new housing built in all areas of the town. The old St Hilda's and Middlesbrough Dock areas have been rebranded "Middlehaven" where the new Middlesbrough College stands and various new, modern office buildings built forming what is known as the Boho Zone, which supports the growing digital sector for which the town has become well established. Where once the old original township stood and heavy industry surrounded, with the dinosaur-like Transporter Bridge spanning the Tees at its northern side, a wave of redevelopment has been taking place to revitalise the area.

New roads and a new dock entrance bridge have opened up the area ready for a planned Snow Centre – a first for the Tees Valley – and more "Boho" buildings are also planned; some have even occupied historic buildings, like the former National and Provincial Bank on the corner of Queen's Square. Other historic buildings still stand in the area, like the Customs House of the 1830s which is now a youth centre, and the original Town Hall which lies derelict hoping for a better future.

In the town centre a new office complex of buildings has being constructed around Combined Courts, Corporation Road and replacing the town lake. Parts of the 1970s Civic Centre has been earmarked for demolition to make way for it.

With the growth of Teesside University, student accommodation blocks proliferate around the town, particularly near Linthorpe Road and Dunning Street, with old office blocks like Teesside House and Rede House converted into accommodation and new blocks being built on Woodlands Road.

Linthorpe Road itself has been revitalised with many independent shops, bars and restaurants emerging. This has also been the case along the formerly unloved Baker and Bedford streets, which have been turned into a thriving hub of small businesses, eateries and entertainment venues.

New hotels have sprung up in the town, like the Holiday Inn Express in the Albert Road frontage of the Cleveland Centre, the Travelodge on the site of the former North Riding Infirmary, and the Premier Inn next to the Jurys Inn (formerly the Dragonara).

Further waves of clearing old Victorian terraces have been experienced in the Gresham area. This will make way for a new Student Village, retail premises and modern housing.

The 2010s have been a tremendous decade of change on a scale not seen since the Victorian building boom when the town was expanding fast. The next decades are sure see even more exciting developments come to fruition, transforming Middlesbrough even further.

2012 saw the Olympic Torch come to Middlesbrough at the beginning of the year which saw London host the Summer Olympic Games. Great crowds followed its journey through various Teesside locations, and especially in Middlesbrough as it crossed the Transporter and came to Centre Square. The population came out in great numbers and especially in support of the local folk who were chosen to carry the Torch through town.

Local lad James Coupland was the first Middlesbrough torchbearer who alighted from the Transporter Bridge carried it for a short distance before handing it on. I myself walked with him along Durham Street.

In Centre Square, a large stage was set up to celebrate the event and to present to the public the local torchbearers before the flame moved on to other parts the country. A vast crowd assembled to see the torch depart.

Middlesbrough folk - especially those born and bred here - are justly proud of "their" Transporter Bridge. With the image here showing it in all its glory, who wouldn't be?

The original "gondala" was in use from the bridge's opening in 1911 until the new larger one, seen here coming in to the Middlesbrough landing, replaced it in 2015.

Local artist Mackenzie Thorpe was commissioned in 2019 to create a bronze sculpture to celebrate the industrial heritage of Teesside. It was installed next to the Transporter Bridge and, according to the artist, acknowledges a time when families would wait for the return of droves of workers who would cross the Tees to work long hard shifts.

A large dual-ringed public art installation named Temenos was unveiled in 2010 alongside the Riverside Stadium and the entrance to the former Middlesbrough Dock. It is by artist Anish Kapoor and structural designer Cecil Balmond. Temenos is the Greek word for a sanctuary or a holy area cut off from its surroundings.

Temenos seen here in this evening view is juxtaposed with the Transporter Bridge and old dock tower in the background.

A remarkable reminder of the industry once located in the St Hilda's area of Middlesbrough is the Vulcan Street Wall, which once belonged to the Cleveland Salt Works. This area was also home to much industry with droves of townsfolk working long hard shifts in the heavy industries all around.

The first Bolckow & Vaughan ironworks, Middlesbrough Pottery and the salt works were located in the area behind the imposing wall. Today it remains preserved with the Transporter Bridge as a backdrop.

Seen here is the site of the former St Hilda's Church, with the old town hall in the background. This area was once the thriving heart of Middlesbrough, set around the Market Square, all of which has long since disappeared. St Hilda's was the first parish church of the town, but was demolished in 1969. The future of the derelict town hall is not certain. Built in 1846, it is one of the oldest surviving structures in Middlesbrough.

Another beacon of Middlesbrough's past still standing today is the former Customs House on North Street in the St Hilda's area. Built in the 1830s, it served as a business exchange, meeting hall and hotel. It was transformed into myplace – an activity and leisure centre for young people in 2011.

The dock tower presently standing on its own will be joined by the proposed snow dome centre by 2022 if the current plans come to fruition. It was once a prominent landmark for approaching ships, and also provided hydraulic power for operating the dock gates and cranes. It was restored in 2005.

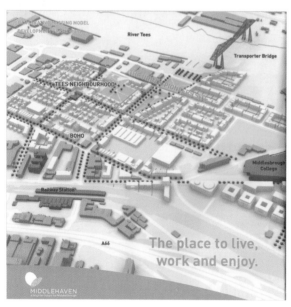

The new plan for Middlehaven seen here was unveiled in 2014 in a blaze of publicity, and since its implementation progress has been slow but construction has begun with many new buildings already completed. These include the Middlesbrough College, various homes, the Middlesbrough Police headquarters, a sixth form college, and various Boho buildings. Future projects planned are the snow centre, offices, apartments, housing, a secondary school and projected relocation of the Middlesbrough College of Art. The Urban Pioneers site is working to beautify and develop the approach from the town to the Transporter Bridge.

Victorian buildings such as these were typical of the old town. These were the last row of such structures left standing along Bridge Street East, demolished in 2019.

The former Masham Hotel on the corner of Vaughan Street and Linthorpe Road was a favourite drinking establishment in the town. Although now operating as a retail unit, the listed building retains much of the classic features of its former life, including the sign above the corner window, the green tiled exterior and Bass logos under the windows.

The brand new Middlesbrough HQ of Cleveland Police was built on Bridge Street West on derelict land which had formerly been the site of St Mary's Roman Catholic Cathedral in the St Hilda's area.

As the St Hilda's area undergoes the latest round of redevelopment works, new housing and a landscaped area have been built alongside Durham Street. It has opened up an impressive vista linking the Transporter Bridge with the rest of the town.

The new Middlesbrough College was built on land 'Over the Border' in what had become known as Middlehaven. The large single campus was designed to merge previous colleges spread around the town. Construction of the £68 million building began in 2007 and opened the following year, now providing a centre for education in this revitalised part of the town.

The award-winning design, as seen here from across the old Middlesbrough Dock, is built to reflect a ship's hull, with a wave-shaped roof and glass-and-metal cladding. It reflects the history of the shipbuilding and former docks close by.

The college's main entrance is located on Dock Street. An impressive internal 'street' runs through the entire length of the building.

Viewed from the dockside roadway the college is flanked by the old dock tower with a scenic dockside walkway to enjoy.

On the south side of the former Middlesbrough Dock, the Hudson Quay offices were built as part of the Middlehaven plan. They represent the early fruition of the council's vision for the redevelopment of the area.

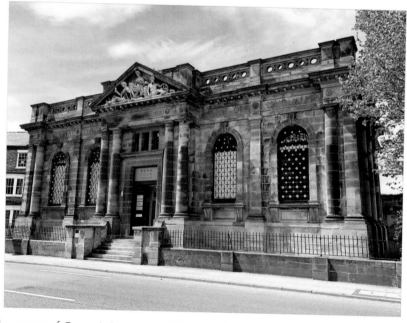

On the corner of Queen's Square and Cleveland Street is the former National Provincial Bank built in 1872. This classical structure is a famous landmark in the town and has recently been brought into the new Boho Zone and renamed Gibson House following a £1 million makeover. It is now home to firms involved in creative and digital businesses.

The new Boho Zone inaugurated by the council as a creative digital cluster of buildings to stimulate development of the old St. Hilda's area has now expanded to incorporate the buildings in Exchange Square and the old Crown House on Linthorpe Road. The success of the scheme has culminated in more buildings being planned.

Boho One is seen here alongside the famous Club Bongo International on Bridge Street West. The Boho Zone was created by Middlesbrough Council to develop the growing digital media and technology sector within the town by providing purpose-built high-quality office spaces.

One of the latest buildings to be added is the Boho Five in Middlehaven. Located close to the railway line and near Middlesbrough College, this business building has 50 up-to-date and modern office units.

The Grange Road entrance to the Cleveland Centre. It is still the most popular shopping precinct in the heart of the town centre and home to many of the national chain stores such as Boots, WH Smith and Iceland.

Modern attractive signage was added to various town centre locations to guide locals as well as visitors. Seen here is one of these markers on the corner of Linthorpe Road and Borough Road.

Baker Street and Bedford Street in the centre of the town had lain unloved for decades but were given a new lease of life when Middlesbrough Council had the old houses refurbished into new retail premises. Now they are home to a thriving collection of independent shops, bars and other businesses which attract people from far and wide and have become a new retail destination.

Streets of terraced housing in the Gresham area of Middlesbrough have been sequentially boarded up and then demolished as the next phase of the town centre's redevelopment takes place. However, the project has stalled a number of times, leaving unattractive scenes of dereliction. The future of the area is as a student village with open spaces and higher quality residential accommodation.

Numbers 6, 8 and 10 Ruby Street now stand boarded up awaiting their final demolition, which is planned by early 2020.

A 40-metre high big wheel was erected in Centre Square seen in early 2010 as Middlesbrough entered the next decade. It offered incredible views over the town as far away as Teesport and the Cleveland Hills, as well as the surrounding town centre which had changed so much in the past century.

With the development of a new police headquarters for Middlesbrough near the railway station and site of the former St Mary's Cathedral, the old police station on Dunning Road was demolished in June 2010. Seen here being demolished on a wintry day from Emily Street, the site remains undeveloped. A car park now occupies the site.

Teesside University's campus has grown incredibly since the late 1990s. Many new buildings have been constructed and many more are planned. In recent years Southfield Road has been pedestrianized as a central boulevard at the heart of the university's modern collection of buildings.

Teesside University's Library opened in the late 1990s. It is seen here two decades later, having recently undergone a £7 million renovation to keep it relevant and up to date as the focal point of the campus.

The new £7.5 million Business School opened in 2018, with a unique display of foliage on its exterior, making it one of the most popular of the newer buildings.

The elegant King Edward's Square is one of Middlesbrough's most unique student accommodation areas. Formerly two rows of terraced townhouses typical of the early days of Middlesbrough; they have been repurposed into modern living spaces for Teesside University's students set around a tranquil square at the hub of the university buildings.

The Curve building, which opened in 2015. Its innovative architectural design features a gold-coloured exterior and almost 1,500sq metres of teaching space inside. Where it stands on the newly pedestrianised Southfield Road was once rows of terraced houses.

The new Student Life building under construction in 2019.

Melrose House is another obsolete and empty office block sitting derelict and awaiting the wrecking ball. New offices are in the pipeline for this valuable town centre location.

So many new housing developments have been built or planned. Typical of these estates is this one built on the former Clairville Stadium site. These houses face Clairville Common and Albert Park.

Houses boarded up ready for the wrecking ball on the Grove Hill estate are secured by the council against vandalism and arson, with the ubiquitous green metal doors and shutters.

A new Premier Inn hotel on Wilson Street was built on an adjoining site to the much larger Jury's Inn (formerly the Dragonara Hotel).

Once the site of the North Riding Infirmary, the new Travelodge hotel seen in this view commands its position on the corner of Hartington and Newport roads. An Aldi supermarket is part of the same complex.

Much loved, the lovely Town Lake, in the town centre is to be drained and, with parts of Central Gardens, is to be developed with new office buildings. This complex will be one of the largest ever building projects in the town. Two of the seven blocks have been completed at the time of writing, but not yet occupied, however the future beckons.

The new office building that overlooks the lake as viewed from MIMA.

One of the modern office buildings built along The Boulevard in 2019, opposite the Combined Courts.

Another new office block next to the Civic Centre as viewed across the lake from Grange Road. It stands on the site of the former Registry Office.

Seen from the former Russell Street, known now as The Boulevard. The famous Bottle of Notes sculpture adds to the scene.

Acknowledgements

My thanks go to many friends and long-standing local residents, especially Sue & Ron who, like myself, are very proud of their hometown. Sue is the founder of the fantastic Facebook group Memories of Middlesbrough (MoM), as well as being a keen local photographer who chronicles the urban landscape, capturing the town's changes. Her images are second to none, some of which I have used in this book.

Other prominent local friends who have always supported and helped me in my quest for local images are Louise and Zoe from the Dorman Museum. In addition, the staff at Teesside Archives are always ready and willing to assist me in my local research – especially Cori Dales. I would also like to thank the staff at Middlesbrough's Central Library who are always helpful and supportive of my endeavours.

I'd like to thank one of my oldest Middlesbrough friends, an author an local historian with a passion for the town's history – the extremely knowledgeable Paul Stephenson.

I would like to acknowledge my close friend and great travel companion Raja Asghar. Like me, he loved our hometown and often inspired me to carry on my work chronicling the changes. He was an ardent believer in my abilities and very proud of my achievements in pursuit of Middlesbrough's photographic history. He sadly passed away in 2018 and is greatly missed by us all.

I'd like to acknowledge the continued encouragement and support of my Friday night card club friends and take this opportunity to thank them all. The core members include Ashy, Mancha, Nab, Ish, Shab, Shaheen, Talib and Zah.

A very special thanks to my friend Alyas Rahim and his son Haris for their continued belief and unfettered encouragement to complete all that I set out to achieve.

As always offering 110% support are my immediate family, including my elder brother Bari who is Middlesbrough through and through, as is my nephew Khurram even though he now lives 6,000 miles away in California. His American wife Maria now understands our passion for this town having visited several times. Always ready to help in any way are my younger brother Hamed, his wife Karen and their daughter Sofia, plus my loving and caring sister Shahadh.

Always very supportive of my local history interests is my brother's father-in-law, Colin Bage, as was his late wife May. Not forgetting my sister-in-law Masurat for her tireless help in maintaining and safeguarding my photographic collection, an important role she took on from my late mother Nafees Chohan.

More recent proud residents of Middlesbrough include my adoptive, loving son Rizwan (Rizzy) who is my bedrock and whose care, love and support is a godsend. In addition my very loving and caring niece Maqdass and her son Rohan who are always encouraging to me.

Other family and friends who have always been avid supporters of all my work include cousins Lydia Noor and husband Norman in Pocklington, plus Vanda and John Sherwood in Acklam. My trio of cousins in Leicester, Shahbaz, Imtiaz and especially Ejaz. Not forgetting my very caring friends Coleen Jennings and Afzal.

In London my long-standing friends Moni Gill, Tony Coombes and John Monaghan, plus Carol, Bobby, Billy and EM. Shina.

Abroad in the USA are my dearest friend Tahiree and his wonderful wife Shamyla in Houston, and my closest friend and "Brother" Ravi in Washington DC. Sajjid and Jujji in Dubai and my very close cousin Manni and family in Milan. Last but not Least my "family" in Perth WA: Doris and the whole Hankinson clan, especially my "Brother" Glenn, wife Olivia and boys Preston and Brody. My most ardent fans. Also my very close and loving friends who are ex Middlesbrough but now reside in Western Australia, I thank you David and Sandy Smith for your help, love and support over the last 40+ years we have known each other. My New Zealand "family" since 1982 have from the other side of the world never faltered in their love and continued support in all I have undertaken - thank you Alex and Rita Eastwood.

A very special thanks to Matt Falcus, my friend and publisher whose help and support is second to none.

Last but not least, my sincere thanks to all the many folk, both local and worldwide, for their continued and unequivocal support over my almost 54 years of collection old images of Middlesbrough, my birthplace and home town.